Jams&Preserves
Syd Pemberton

Jams&Preserves

Syd Pemberton

PENGUIN BOOKS

PENGUIN BOOKS

Published by the Penguin Group
Penguin Group (Australia)
250 Camberwell Road, Camberwell, Victoria 3124, Australia
(a division of Pearson Australia Group Pty Ltd)
Penguin Group (USA) Inc.
375 Hudson Street, New York, New York 10014, USA
Penguin Group (Canada)
90 Eglinton Avenue East, Suite 700, Toronto ON M4P 2Y3, Canada
(a division of Pearson Penguin Canada Inc.)
Penguin Books Ltd
80 Strand, London WC2R 0RL, England
Penguin Ireland
25 St Stephen's Green, Dublin 2, Ireland
(a division of Penguin Books Ltd)
Penguin Books India Pvt Ltd
11 Community Centre, Panchsheel Park, New Delhi – 110 017, India
Penguin Group (NZ)
Cnr Airborne and Rosedale Roads, Albany, Auckland, New Zealand
(a division of Pearson New Zealand Ltd)
Penguin Books (South Africa) (Pty) Ltd
24 Sturdee Avenue, Rosebank, Johannesburg 2196, South Africa

Penguin Books Ltd, Registered Offices: 80 Strand, London, WC2R 0RL, England

First published by Penguin Group (Australia), 2006

10 9 8 7 6 5 4 3 2 1

Design by Jay Ryves © Penguin Group (Australia)
Cover photographs by Georgie Cole
Cover styling by Opel Khan
Penguin Books would like to thank Orson & Blake and Michael A Greene Antiques for kindly lending
their merchandise for the cover photographs.
Typeset in New York and Akzidenz Grotesk by Post Pre-press Group, Brisbane, Queensland
Printed and bound in Australia by McPherson's Printing Group, Maryborough, Victoria

National Library of Australia
Cataloguing-in-Publication data:

Pemberton, Syd.
  Jams & preserves.
  Includes index.
  ISBN 0 14 300361 5.
  1. Jam. 2. Sauces. 3. Chutney. I. Title.

641.852

www.penguin.com.au

Contents

Introduction

This book covers jams, marmalades and jellies, pickles and chutneys, as well as ketchups, vinegars, sauces, syrups, curds and a few other unusual fruit and vegetable preserves.

When I began gathering recipes for this book, I was excited by the many delicious preserves I could fill my pantry with, as well as by the marvellous array of gifts I could shower upon friends and relatives who had followed the progress of my experimenting with fruits, sugars, vinegars and spices.

Many years ago I made preserves for delicatessens and cafes. I spent long hours in a commercial kitchen slicing eggplants, grilling capsicums, peeling onions and then hot-filling lots of jars that were then sterilised in a steam oven. Making preserves in your home kitchen is rewarding, but keep the quantities realistic. The challenge of processing large boxes of fruit and vegetables before they go off will be overwhelming unless you have a kitchen set up for it!

This book has been a joy to research and write. I spent many weeks reading and experimenting, and came to the conclusion that preserving is an art – so much depends on the produce (I used seasonal, organic produce wherever possible), equipment and, of course, the balance of flavours. It is an art that requires time and patience, but the end result can be very rewarding.

Enthusiasts who make preserves from their own garden produce every year, or who love to bottle something special when there is a glut at the local market, will find some new and interesting recipes to try. Even the novice will find the recipes easy to follow, and the results of their experiments may well become favourites with family and friends.

A special thanks to the Chadwick family who seemed to give me an endless supply of jars in return for something for their pantry! Also, a big thanks to all the tasters – Sarah, Barry and Ian – who generously spread toast with the jams and marmalades and then returned all the empty jars!

Equipment

To make preserves you will need a few kitchen tools. Not all the things listed here are necessary, but they will certainly make the task a little easier. If you are serious about making preserves, investing in good equipment is essential.

A good preserving pan – should be wide to allow for rapid boiling and evaporation so that the setting point will be reached more quickly. It should hold at least 13 litres and needs to be heavy-based to ensure even heat distribution and to prevent burning or sticking. Stainless steel, aluminium, and good-quality enamel are recommended for making sweet chutneys, pickles, jams and marmalades. A smaller saucepan (preferably 8–10 litres) can be used for cooking small amounts. Special brass and copper preserving pans may be used, but must be very clean and have no trace of polish; they should not be used for pickles or chutneys as the vinegar reacts with the metal and spoils the preserve.

Spoons – ones with long handles are best as they won't slip into the pan and will also keep your hands away from the boiling liquid. Wooden and stainless steel spoons are excellent, and a slotted spoon will remove scum or pips from the surface of jams and marmalades. Measuring spoons for ingredients are also essential.

Knives – a couple of good sharp kitchen knives, a large chef's knife for chopping and another for paring vegetables or fruit

Scales – essential for measuring produce, sugar and other ingredients used in large amounts

Ladle – a couple of metal ladles of different sizes, one with a lip for easy pouring

Jugs – measuring jug and cups, and a metal or glass pouring jug for filling jars

Muslin – for tying up pips, stones and spices; also for straining preserves

Kitchen string – for tying the muslin bags

Wooden board – to stand the hot jars on during filling. It also provides a safe surface while the jars are cooling down – the timber insulates the jars from cold or damp surfaces, which could crack the glass.

Sugar thermometer – for measuring the temperatures for setting point. Jams and jellies set at just below 105°C, when the sugar interacts with the acid and natural fruit pectin.

Citrus juicer – to extract juices from lemons, oranges, limes, tangerines, grapefruit and any other citrus used for making marmalade and jam

Nylon sieve – a non-corrosive tool for sieving acidic foods

Citrus zester – to remove the skin only and not the bitter pith

Jelly bag – to strain fruit or vegetables for jellies. The traditional cloth jelly bag is conical in shape, with four attachments for hanging it up. It is first dampened with boiling water, then suspended between four legs of a chair over a bowl below and usually left overnight for the juice to drip through slowly. These seem to be scarce so make your own out of good-quality light canvas.

Another way of sieving the fruit pulp is to line a conical sieve with cloth and to suspend it over a bowl. Once the liquid has dripped through, strain again with another clean wet cloth over a bowl.

Funnels – make it easier to accurately fill jars when pouring in hot preserves. They are usually plastic or stainless steel and come in a variety of sizes.

Electric food processor – for finely chopping or pureeing food. A hand-held electric blender can be used directly in the preserving pan and is often easier to clean.

Rubber kitchen or gardening gloves – good for holding hot jars when screwing on lids or for transferring hot jars to a cooling-down board. Use good-quality rubber.

Jars and bottles – these can be in a variety of sizes, but use larger ones for produce that will be eaten up quickly and smaller jars for something special. They must be sterilised before use. Jars with screw-top metal lids are best for most preserves, except for pickles or chutneys with high vinegar content. There are special preserving jars with a rubber seal and wire clip for the lids. Jars with wide mouths are easier to fill. Clear covers are available at some supermarkets and can be used instead of a metal lid. Corks can be used for bottles, but make sure they are inserted while the preserve is still hot.

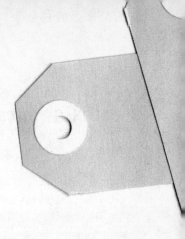

The basics

The preserving of foods developed mainly to keep store cupboards full of produce out of season. Sugar, vinegar, salt and alcohol were used, and still are today. Though nowadays, with excellent canned, frozen and dried foods available, the practice is not as widespread.

Each recipe contains specific instructions, though there are some general principles that apply to all preserves.

Sterilising jars

Jars must be sterilised before filling, and there are a number of ways to do this. I find the best way is to wash them and dry them off in the oven just before filling, but you may prefer one of the other methods listed below. Whichever method you choose, you must first thoroughly wash, rinse and dry the jars and lids. Note that only the jars are sterilised.

Oven sterilising – preheat oven to 160°C. Place rinsed jars, still wet, on baking trays in the oven for 10 minutes. Remove and cover jars with a clean tea-towel.

Stove-top sterilising – lay a tea-towel or thick paper handtowel in the bottom of a large pan (this protects the jars). Place clean jars on their side in the pan. Cover with water and bring to the boil. Boil for 20 minutes. Take the pan off the heat and cool a little before removing the jars with tongs. Drain well and cover with a clean tea-towel.

Dishwasher sterilising – place jars in a dishwasher and run it on the rinse cycle at the hottest temperature.

Microwave sterilising – place the clean, rinsed jars in the microwave and heat on high for 3 minutes.

Preserving by hot-water bath

Sometimes it is necessary to sterilise the preserve itself because the recipe is low in sugar, acid or vinegar (which normally inhibit the growth of bacteria). In the past, whole fruits and vegetables were commonly preserved by using a hot-water bath. Nowadays, with freezers and fast international transport, fruits and vegetables are available all year round and the pressure to preserve with this method has declined. However, if you are serious about bottling fruits and vegetables, a special sterilising kit is a good investment.

When processing in a hot-water bath, there are a few points to remember:

o When filling the jars, keep 2 cm at the top to allow the contents to rise when heated.

o Place a cloth or thick wads of newspaper or paper towel in the base of a saucepan to protect the bottom of the jars.

o Wrap newspaper or paper towel around each bottle, secured with a rubber band, to protect it from hitting the other bottles during boiling.

o Foods that are to be processed from cold must go into cold water, which is then brought up to the boil.

o Hot-filled preserves must go into hot water, which is then brought up to the boil.

o The water must be brought very slowly to the boil (reaching 92°C in 45–60 minutes), and this temperature maintained for approximately 30 minutes. (See individual recipes for the exact processing time.)

o Allow jars to cool slightly before removing and placing on wooden cooling boards.

o Check each jar to see that a vacuum has formed.

o Allow jars to cool completely before labelling.

Pectin

Pectin is the natural gum-like substance found in all fruits and some vegetables. It is essential in fruit preserves such as jams, jellies and marmalades as it reacts with the sugar to help the mixture set. It is normally at its highest when fruit is just beginning to ripen. For fruit with little or no pectin, the pips and pith of high-pectin fruits (usually citrus) are often included during cooking. A commercial jam setting powder can be used instead of adding high-pectin fruits. Commercial pectin is also available in liquid form.

1 Overripe fruit is low in pectin.
2 Freshly picked fruit will be high in pectin; the longer the fruit is stored the more pectin will be lost.
3 Frozen fruit is lower in pectin than fresh produce.

Fruit pectin levels		
Poor	Medium	High
cherries	apricots	currants (red, black, white)
strawberries	blackberries	cranberries
pears	raspberries	lemons
figs	plums	quinces
mulberries	peaches	cumquats
rhubarb	grapes	grapefruit
nectarines	tomatoes	oranges
melons	apples	Seville oranges
pineapples	blueberries	tangerines
passionfruit	prickly pear	
guava		
bananas		
tamarillos		
feijoa		

Acid

Like pectin, the acid in fruit reacts with the sugars to help the jam set. To balance jams, jellies and marmalades, high-acid fruits can be combined with low-acid fruits.

Low-acid fruits include strawberries, pears, cherries (sweet varieties), figs, kiwi fruit, mangoes, melons, pineapples and tomatoes: they require the addition of 2 tablespoons of lemon juice for every 2 kg of fruit. Citric acid can be added at 1 teaspoon per 2 kg of fruit.

In chutneys, pickles and other preserves, vinegar (acetic acid) helps to preserve the fruit and vegetables so that sterilisation by hot-water bath is not required. The vinegar should contain 5–6 per cent acetic acid.

Testing for setting point

When the sugar has been added to the fruit, the mixture is then brought to a hard boil. When testing whether the jam, jelly or marmalade has reached setting point, always remember to check earlier rather than later, and to remove the pot from the heat while you check. Note that smaller amounts will reach setting point faster than larger amounts.

There are several ways to test for setting point:

1 **A thermometer** – when the jam reaches 105–110°C (221–230°F) it will be ready to set.

2 **The saucer test** – remove a small amount of mixture with a spoon and drop onto a cold saucer brought from the freezer or refrigerator. Push a finger across the top of the jam as it cools: if the skin wrinkles, the mixture is ready to set.

3 **The spoon test** – take a wooden spoon and stir the jam. Remove the spoon, allow the jam to cool slightly, then tip the spoon so the jam runs off. If the jam forms a flake and will not drop off unless shaken, it has reached setting point.

Presentation and storage

To allow whole fruit or shredded peel to be evenly distributed through the jam or marmalade, cool the mixture before spooning into the prepared jars. (Fruit or peel rises to the top if it is not cooled before potting.)

Any scum that forms on the surface can be scooped off with a slotted spoon at the point of setting. However scum does not affect the flavour of the jam or marmalade, only the look and possibly the clarity – if you are entering a jam-making competition you'll be marked down for this, but no one at home will care!

Always store preserves in a dark, dry place. Light will oxidise fruit and vegetables and the preserve will darken. Once opened, always store jam, jelly or marmalade in the refrigerator. Chutneys and pickles should be kept in a cool, dark place for 1–2 months before use, to allow the flavours to mature. Some can be stored in the refrigerator (see individual recipes).

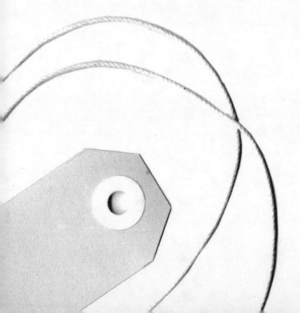

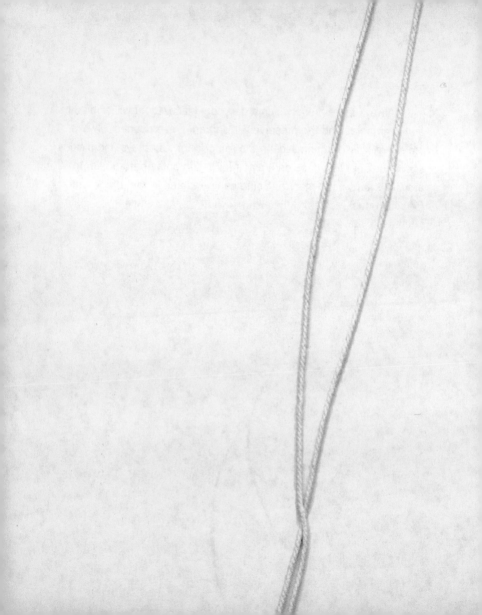

Jams

Jam making is a great way to use up seasonal fruits. Understanding the method of jam making is essential when following the recipes in this book.

- Try to select slightly under-ripe fruit where possible, except when using apples, as overripe fruits will be low in pectin. Fruits naturally low in pectin will need it added in the form of pips, pith, citrus fruits, apple or lemon juice, or commercial pectin (jam setting mixture).

- Granulated white sugar is the main sugar used in jam making. Dark or raw sugar is not used as it can change the colour of the fruit.

- Dry fruit like pears or apples need water to help them cook. Fruit such as strawberries or raspberries need less water.

- Adding about a tablespoon of butter with the sugar will prohibit scum forming on the jam.

Strawberry and rhubarb jam with a hint of roses

Strawberries are sometimes at their best in winter and marry well with rhubarb. The rosewater adds a little taste of Morocco to this jam.

Makes approximately 4 × 225 g jars

500 g under-ripe strawberries, hulled

500 g rhubarb, trimmed, washed and chopped into small chunks

3 lemons, juice extracted and pips tied in muslin

650 g white granulated sugar

¼–½ teaspoon rosewater

In a mixing bowl layer the strawberries, rhubarb, lemon juice and pips and sugar. Leave overnight.

Transfer all the ingredients (except the pips) to a preserving pan and slowly bring to the boil. Cook at a fast boil until setting point is reached. Remove from heat and stir in the rosewater. Pour into warm, sterilised jars and seal.

Strawberry jam with Grand Marnier

Use very firm strawberries if you wish to keep them whole.
Stir gently so as not to break up the fruit.

Makes approximately 7 × 375 g jars

1 kg firm, ripe strawberries, hulled

1.5 kg white granulated sugar

1 cup (250 ml) water

2 tablespoons Grand Marnier

juice of 1 small lemon

Place the sugar and water in a preserving pan and stir over a medium heat until the sugar has dissolved. Bring to the boil and simmer for 15 minutes. Remove from heat, add the whole strawberries, and set aside for 10 minutes to allow the strawberry juices to be drawn out.

Pour the Grand Marnier into a clean bowl. Remove the strawberries from the sugar syrup and add to the Grand Marnier. Gently stir through. Bring the syrup back to the boil and cook for a further 10 minutes. Pour the strawberries back into the pan, add the lemon juice and return to the boil. Cook for 2–4 minutes. Remove from heat and scoop any scum from the top. Spoon jam into warm, sterilised jars and seal.

Whole strawberry jam

Makes approximately 3 × 500 g jars

800 g strawberries, hulled

1 kg white granulated sugar

juice of 1 lime

juice of 1 lemon

2 tablespoons jam setter
(see page 11)

Place the strawberries, sugar, lime juice and lemon juice in
a preserving pan. Heat gently until the sugar has dissolved.
Stir in the jam setter and bring to the boil. Cook for 5 minutes.
Remove the fruit with a slotted spoon and place in sterilised jars.
Boil the syrup a further 10 minutes until reduced. Cool syrup a little
before pouring over the strawberries. Seal immediately.

Pomegranate jam

This is an interesting jam. If the seeds are not sieved it can be a little crunchy in texture.

Makes approximately 3 × 250 g jars

1 kg (approx) pomegranates (gives about 500 g of fruit once seeds removed)

grated rind of 1 orange

125 ml orange juice

125 ml water

2 tablespoons lemon juice

500 g white granulated sugar, warmed

Score the skin of each pomegranate into quarters with a sharp stainless steel knife. Break open the fruit into quarters and carefully dislodge the seeds from the membrane.

Place all the ingredients in a preserving pan and slowly bring to the boil over a low heat, stirring from time to time. Cook at a simmer for about 20 minutes until setting point is reached. Remove from heat, spoon into warm, sterilised jars and seal.

To make a pomegranate jelly, cook the ingredients for 10 minutes. Sieve the jam (push the mixture through a sieve, leaving the seeds behind) and cook for a further 10 minutes or until setting point is reached.

Blackberry jam

Blackberries are in season for a short time and make a lovely jam. It is best to use fruit that is just ripe to get the best flavour.

Makes approximately 4 × 225 g jars

600 g blackberries

2 teaspoons lemon juice

2 tablespoons water

250 g white granulated sugar

Place all the ingredients in a preserving pan and slowly bring to the boil, stirring gently. Boil for 10–15 minutes until setting point is reached. Remove from heat and skim off any scum. Spoon the jam into warm, sterilised jars and seal.

Plum jam

Makes approximately 4 × 225 g jars

1 kg plums, halved and
stones removed

600 g white granulated sugar

Place the plum stones in a mortar and pestle in batches and gently crush them. Transfer to a muslin bag and tie securely.

Place the halved plums in a stainless steel bowl with the sugar and bag of crushed stones. Cover and leave overnight in a cool place.

Transfer plums, sugar and stones to a preserving pan and slowly bring to the boil, stirring gently. Cook for 25–35 minutes, removing any scum with a spoon as the jam reaches setting point. Take off the heat and remove the stones, gently squeezing out the juice. Spoon the jam into warm, sterilised jars and seal.

Apricot jam with almonds

Makes approximately 5 × 250 g jars

750 g firm, ripe apricots, halved
  and stones removed

350 g white granulated sugar

200 ml water

2 teaspoons lemon juice

50 g flaked blanched almonds

Place apricots in a stainless steel bowl with the sugar, water and lemon juice, and set aside for 6 hours.

Transfer apricot mixture to a preserving pan and bring gently to the boil. Boil rapidly until setting point is reached. Remove from heat and stir in the blanched almonds. Spoon the jam into warm, sterilised jars and seal.

Plum jam with Cointreau

Makes approximately 5 × 225 g jars

1.5 kg plums, halved and
  stones removed

375 ml water

750 g white granulated sugar

1½ tablespoons lemon juice

⅓ cup Cointreau *or* Grand Marnier

Place the plum halves in a preserving pan with the water and cook over a gentle heat until soft (10–15 minutes). Puree in a blender or food processor and return to the pan with the sugar and lemon juice. Slowly bring to the boil and cook for 10–20 minutes until setting point is reached. Stir in the Cointreau and cook for 1 minute. Remove from heat, spoon into warm, sterilised jars and seal.

Fresh fig jam with star anise

This is a delicious preserve – the star anise adds a lovely fragrance to the classic Middle Eastern fruit.

Makes 4 × 175 g jars

600 g ripe green figs, cut into quarters

300 g white granulated sugar

125 ml water

grated rind of 1 lemon

2 whole star anise

¼ teaspoon Chinese five-spice powder

Place figs in a stainless steel bowl with the sugar and leave overnight in a cool place.

Transfer to a preserving pan with the water, lemon rind, star anise and Chinese five-spice powder. Bring to the boil over a gentle heat and boil for 20–30 minutes until setting point. Remove from heat, pour into warm, sterilised jars and seal.

Slow-roasted tomato and almond jam

Makes approximately 4 × 200 g jars

1 kg slow-roasted tomatoes (see page 119)

250 g cherry tomatoes, chopped

800 g white granulated sugar

grated rind of 2 lemons

juice of 1½ lemons

70 g flaked blanched almonds

Place the slow-roasted tomatoes, cherry tomatoes, sugar, lemon rind and lemon juice in a preserving pan. Slowly dissolve the sugar over a low heat, stirring occasionally. Bring to the boil and cook until setting point (20–30 minutes). Remove from heat and cool for 10 minutes. Spoon jam into warm, sterilised jars and seal.

Feijoa jam

Makes 3 × 250 g jars

1 kg feijoa, peeled and sliced

¾ cup water

juice and rind of 1 lemon

600 g white granulated sugar

Place the sliced feijoas and water in a preserving pan and slowly bring to the boil. Simmer for 20 minutes until the fruit is pulpy. Add the lemon juice, rind and sugar. Bring slowly to the boil and cook until setting point is reached. Remove from heat, pour into warm, sterilised jars and seal.

Black cherry jam

Makes approximately 6 × 250 g jars

1 kg firm black cherries
   (not overripe)

750 g white granulated sugar

¼ cup lemon juice

Pit the cherries (catching any juice) and tie the stones in a muslin bag. Place the cherries, cherry juice and stones in a bowl. Stir in the sugar and allow to stand overnight in a cool place.

Transfer cherry mixture to a preserving pan with the lemon juice and stones. Bring to the boil over a low heat, stirring from time to time, and cook until setting point is reached. Remove the stones and allow the jam to cool slightly. Pour into warm, sterilised jars and seal.

Raspberry jam

Makes approximately 4 × 500 g jars

1 kg raspberries   1 kg white granulated sugar

Combine the raspberries and sugar in a preserving pan and allow to stand overnight in a cool place.

Place pan over a low heat and cook until the sugar has dissolved. Bring to the boil and simmer until setting point is reached. Skim off any scum. Remove from heat, pour into warm, sterilised jars and seal.

If you want a smooth jam, heat the raspberries before adding the sugar until the juices run and the fruit is very soft. Remove from heat and place in a fine plastic sieve, carefully pressing the juice through and leaving the pips behind. Place the raspberry juice and sugar in a preserving pan and follow the cooking instructions above.

Fig, tomato and red onion jam

Makes approximately 6 × 250 g jars

2 tablespoons olive oil

600 g red onions, thinly sliced

4 tablespoons dark brown sugar

5 tablespoons balsamic vinegar

1.5 kg tomatoes, peeled and
roughly chopped

500 g dried figs, sliced

¾ cup lemon juice

1 tablespoon salt

700 g white granulated sugar

Preheat oven to 200°C.

Place the oil in a baking tray and heat in the oven. Stir in the sliced onions and bake for 15 minutes. Remove from the oven and stir in the brown sugar and 2 tablespoons of the balsamic vinegar. Cook for a further 15 minutes until caramelised.

Meanwhile, place the tomatoes, figs, lemon juice and salt in a preserving pan and heat gently for 20 minutes, stirring occasionally, until the tomatoes are soft. Stir the onions into the tomato mixture. Add the white sugar and dissolve over a low heat. Bring to the boil and cook until setting point is reached (about 20 minutes). Stir in the rest of the vinegar and cook for 2–3 minutes. Remove from heat, pour into warm, sterilised jars and seal.

Watermelon and ginger jam

Makes approximately 3 × 750 g jars

500 g trimmed watermelon rind
   (weighed when green skin has
   been cut away)

2 tablespoons sea salt

1 litre water

2 cups white granulated sugar

1 lemon, very thinly sliced

25 g fresh ginger, peeled
   and grated

Cut the watermelon rind into small squares. Place in a bowl and
stir through the salt. Leave for 24 hours. Drain and rinse thoroughly.

In a preserving pan bring the water to the boil. Add the melon
rind and cook for 15–20 minutes until tender. Drain. Reserve 600 ml
of the liquid and return to the pan with the sugar. Bring to the boil and
cook for 10 minutes until syrupy. Add the sliced lemon, melon rind
and grated ginger to the sugar syrup. Bring to the boil and cook for
15 minutes. Remove from heat, pour into warm, sterilised jars
and seal.

Pineapple, tomato and galangal jam

Galangal, also known as Siamese ginger, adds a spicy citrus flavour to this jam. If you can't get galangal use fresh ginger.

Makes approximately 4 × 250 g jars

250 ml freshly squeezed citrus juice (orange, lemon, lime and tangelo), pips reserved

2 medium pineapples, skin removed and flesh finely chopped

1 kg tomatoes, peeled and chopped

2 tablespoons freshly grated galangal

4 whole star anise

700 g white granulated sugar

Tie the citrus pips in a muslin bag. Place in a preserving pan with citrus juice, pineapple, tomatoes, galangal and star anise. Cover and slowly bring to the boil until the tomatoes are soft and pulpy. Add the sugar, stirring until it has dissolved. Bring to the boil and cook until setting point is reached. Remove the muslin bag, squeezing out any juices. Remove jam from heat, pour into warm, sterilised jars and seal.

Hot-sweet red capsicum jam

For those who like spice at breakfast this makes an interesting jam to start the day! Jalapeño chillies are usually available in the late autumn and can be grown in a pot in a sunny spot.

Makes approximately 5 × 400 g jars

500 g red capsicum, deseeded and cored

100 g fresh jalapeño chillies, deseeded and pith removed

375 ml cider vinegar

1 teaspoon salt

1.3 kg white granulated sugar

50 g jam setter

Place the capsicum and chillies in a food processor with a little of the vinegar. Process until finely chopped. Transfer to a preserving pan with the rest of the vinegar and the salt. Bring to the boil over a medium heat and simmer for about 5 minutes. Remove from heat and check if the mixture measures 3 cups: if not, add some freshly squeezed lime or lemon juice. Return to the pan and add the sugar and jam setter. Stir to mix well, then bring to a rolling boil and cook for about 5 minutes. Remove from heat, pour into warm, sterilised jars and seal.

Rhubarb and raspberry jam

Makes approximately 3 × 500 g jars

500 g rhubarb, washed, trimmed
and diced

600 g white granulated sugar

300 g raspberries (use frozen
when not in season)

2 tablespoons lemon juice

Place rhubarb in a mixing bowl, sprinkle with sugar and leave overnight
to extract the juices.

Gently heat the rhubarb mixture in a preserving pan until all the
sugar has dissolved and then add the raspberries and lemon juice.
Bring to the boil and cook until setting point is reached (about
20 minutes). Remove from heat, pour into warm, sterilised jars
and seal.

Tamarillo jam

Also known as tree tomatoes, tamarillos make delicious jam.
Like raspberries, tamarillos only have a short season, so
make plenty of this jam!

Makes approximately 4 × 350 g jars

1 kg tamarillos

1 cup water

600 g white granulated sugar

juice of 1 lemon, pips reserved
and tied in muslin

Plunge the tamarillos into a bowl of hot water for 3–4 minutes, then
remove the skins. Roughly chop the flesh and place in a preserving
pan with the water and lemon pips. Slowly bring to the boil and cook
for 8–10 minutes until the fruit is soft. Stir in the sugar and lemon
juice and heat slowly until dissolved. Bring to the boil and cook until
setting point is reached. Remove from heat, pour into warm, sterilised
jars and seal.

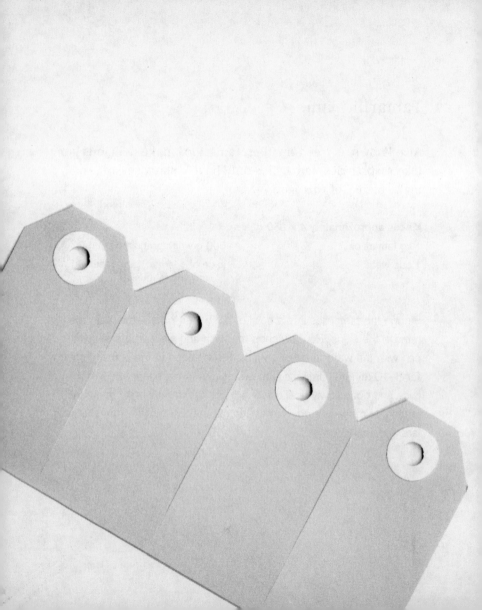

Jellies

Jelly making is similar to jam, except for the draining of the fruit through a jelly bag. The magnificent clear, bright jelly is certainly worth the effort.

o   Use perfect fruit without any bruising or damage. There's no need to peel it, just chop it into chunks.

o   The amount of sugar needed to make a jelly is calculated by measuring the fruit syrup after straining. Usually 2 cups of sugar is needed for every 600 ml of liquid.

o   Use just enough water to cover the fruit, then cook until the fruit is soft and can be mashed with a spoon.

o   Make sure the jelly bag is wet before straining the fruit. Although a jelly bag is the best way of getting the juice from the cooked fruit, a wet muslin cloth lining a conical sieve will work just as well. (See page 5 for more on jelly bags.)

o   Testing for setting point is the same as for jams, but test jellies early as they set quicker than jams.

o   If any scum appears, just remove with a slotted spoon before setting. Do not add butter as this will spoil the clarity of the jelly.

Tomato jelly with French tarragon

Makes approximately 3 × 250 g jars

1.4 kg tomatoes, chopped

1 apple, chopped

500 ml water

5 sprigs marjoram

white granulated sugar
(for quantity see below)

1 teaspoon salt

4 tablespoons red wine

a few sprigs fresh
French tarragon

Place tomatoes and apple in a preserving pan with the water and sprigs of marjoram. Bring to the boil and cook until the tomatoes and apple are soft (about 10–15 minutes). Pour into a jelly bag suspended over a bowl, allowing the juices to drip through for at least 4–5 hours, or overnight.

Measure the juice and return to the pan. Add 450 g of sugar for every 600 ml of juice. Bring to the boil and cook until setting point is reached. Stir in the salt and red wine and cook for a further 1–2 minutes. Remove from heat. Place sprigs of tarragon into warm, sterilised jars. Pour in the jelly, and seal.

Apple and rosemary jelly

Makes approximately 6 × 400 g jars

1.5 kg green apples, roughly
    chopped

5 cups water

2½ cups white wine vinegar

white granulated sugar
    (for quantity see below)

½ cup fresh rosemary leaves

extra sprigs of rosemary

In a preserving pan combine the apples, water and vinegar. Bring to the boil and cook 10–15 minutes until the apples are soft. Pour into a jelly bag suspended over a bowl, allowing the juices to drip through for at least 4–5 hours, or overnight.

Measure the juice and return it to the pan. Add 450 g of sugar for every 600 ml of juice. Stir in the rosemary leaves, bring to the boil and cook until setting point. Remove from heat and strain. Place a sprig of rosemary in each warm, sterilised jar, pour in jelly and seal.

To make other herb jellies substitute ½ cup of finely chopped herb leaves for the rosemary, but stir them into the apple mixture when setting point is reached.

Guava jelly

The lime zest gives this delicate jelly a lovely flavour.
Use pink guavas when available and leave out the lime
if preferred.

Makes approximately 4 × 260 g jars

980 g white guavas, chopped

300 ml water

white granulated sugar
(for quantity see below)

juice and grated zest of 1 lime

Place the chopped guavas and the water in a preserving pan and bring
to the boil. Cook for 15–20 minutes until soft. Pour into a jelly bag
suspended over a bowl, allowing the juices to drip through for at least
4–5 hours, or overnight.

Measure the juice and return it to the pan. Add approximately
450 g of sugar for every 600 ml of juice. Stir in the lime juice and
zest, slowly bring to the boil and cook until setting point is reached.
Remove from heat, pour into warm, sterilised jars and seal.

Rose geranium jelly

This beautifully fragranced herb makes a lovely jelly to serve with desserts, over fruit and with Moroccan-style savoury grills. The rose scent permeates the jelly but is not as strong or intense as rosewater.

Makes approximately 6 × 400 g jars

1.5 kg green apples, roughly chopped

1.5 litres of water

25 small rose geranium leaves, washed

white granulated sugar (for quantity see below)

juice of 1 lemon

½ cup cider vinegar

extra geranium leaves

Place the apples, water and geranium leaves in a preserving pan and bring to the boil. Cook for 10–15 minutes until the apples are soft. Pour into a jelly bag suspended over a bowl, allowing the juices to drip through for at least 4–5 hours, or overnight.

Measure the juice and return it to the pan. Add 450 g of sugar for every 600 ml of juice. Bring to the boil and cook until setting point is reached. Remove from heat and strain. Place a fresh rose geranium leaf in each warm, sterilised jar, then pour jelly in and seal.

Orange and lime jelly

Use this jelly to glaze fruit tarts or to spoon over poached fruit. Mix with mascarpone to create an interesting accompaniment to cakes or tarts.

Makes approximately 4 × 225 g jars

1 kg green apples, roughly chopped

500 ml water

250 ml freshly squeezed orange and lime juices

white granulated sugar (for quantity see below)

Combine the apples and water in a preserving pan. Bring to the boil and cook for 10–15 minutes until the apples are soft. Pour into a jelly bag suspended over a bowl, allowing the juices to drip through for at least 4–5 hours, or overnight.

Mix in the citrus juices, measure and return to the pan. Add 450 g of sugar for every 600 ml of juice, bring to the boil and cook until setting point is reached. Remove from heat, pour into warm, sterilised jars and seal.

Prickly pear and lime jelly

Sometimes known as Indian fig, the prickly pear is the fruit of a cactus plant. Rubber gloves are a good idea when handling it.

Makes approximately 6 × 300 g jars

10 prickly pears, washed and sliced into rounds

125 ml water

125 ml freshly squeezed lime juice

1.25 kg white granulated sugar

50 g jam setter

zest of 1 lime, finely grated

Place the prickly pear and water in a preserving pan. Slowly bring to the boil over a low heat and cook until the fruit is soft. Mash the fruit and pour into a jelly bag suspended over a bowl, allowing the juices to drip through for at least 4–5 hours, or overnight.

Place the prickly pear liquid, lime juice, sugar and jam setter in the pan. Bring to the boil and cook for 5 minutes. Stir in the lime zest and cook for 2 minutes. Remove from heat, pour into warm, sterilised jars and seal.

Rosemary and capsicum jewels jelly

This attractive, colourful jelly can be served with barbecued roasted meats and poultry. If orange capsicums are in season, add them to the array of jewels!

Makes approximately 6 × 400 g jars

1 small red capsicum, deseeded and finely chopped

1 small yellow capsicum, deseeded and finely chopped

1 small green capsicum, deseeded and finely chopped

2 long red chillies, deseeded and finely chopped

½ teaspoon sea salt

750 ml cider vinegar

1.4 kg white granulated sugar

50 g jam setter

a few sprigs of rosemary

Place the capsicum, chillies, salt, vinegar and sugar in a preserving pan and bring to the boil over a low heat. Simmer for 10 minutes. Stir in the jam setter, return to the boil and cook for 5 minutes. Remove from heat. Place a rosemary sprig in each of the warm, sterilised jars. Pour in the capsicum jelly and seal.

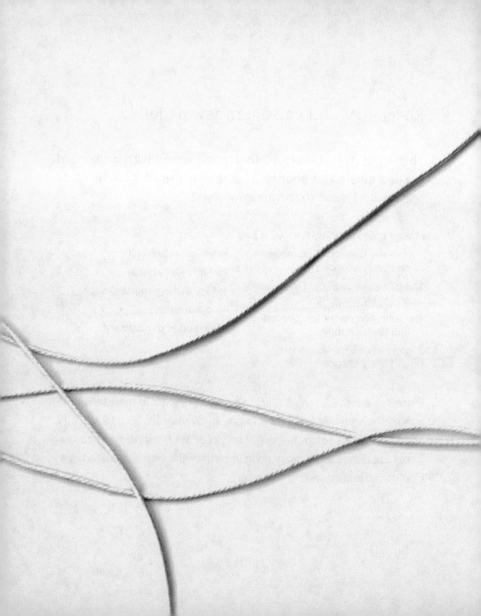

Marmalade is one of my favourite preserves. The method is similar to jam making except that the main ingredients are usually citrus fruits, and the fruit's peel dominates the texture and taste of the marmalade.

- Wash the fruit thoroughly, squeeze the juice and save all the pips for extra pectin.

- Where the fruit is low in acid, adding lemon juice will assist the setting. Recipes will indicate if this is required or not.

- It is important to cook the peel until it is soft. If the sugar is added and the peel is not properly cooked, the skin will toughen.

- Marmalade can go past its setting point and may not set at all if left to boil for too long. Check frequently to see if the mixture is near setting point.

Chunky, bitter-lime marmalade

This is quite a bitter marmalade – spread on wholegrain toast it certainly wakes the palate in the morning!

Makes approximately 6 × 400 g jars

1 kg Tahitian limes
3 litres water

1.5 kg white granulated sugar

Place the whole limes in a preserving pan and cover with the water. Bring to the boil and cook for 1½–2 hours or until the limes are tender. Remove limes from the pan, reserving the water. Allow limes to cool, then cut them in half. Scrape out all the flesh and finely cut up the soft rind.

Place rind in the preserving pan with approximately 2 litres of the cooking water. Bring to the boil and cook until liquid is reduced by half (about 30 minutes). Stir in sugar and dissolve over a low heat. Return to the boil and cook until setting point is reached. Remove from heat, pour into warm, sterilised jars and seal.

Fresh ginger marmalade

Makes approximately 4 × 375 g jars

300 g fresh ginger, peeled and coarsely grated (1½ cups approx)

1.5 litres water

1 tablespoon finely grated lime zest

½ cup fresh lime juice

900 g white granulated sugar

Place the ginger and water in a preserving pan and bring to the boil. Cook for 1½ hours until the ginger is tender. Stir in the lime zest and juice, and the sugar. Bring to the boil over a low heat to dissolve the sugar, then boil the mixture until setting point is reached. Remove from heat and cool the marmalade a little before pouring into warm, sterilised jars and sealing.

Quince marmalade

Makes approximately 6 × 400 g jars

1.5 kg quinces, cored and peeled

zest of 1 orange, finely chopped

zest of 1 lemon, finely chopped

2 cups water

8 cups white granulated sugar

Coarsely grate the quince (in a food processor if you have one). Place the quince, orange and lemon zest, water and sugar in a preserving pan and slowly bring to the boil, stirring occasionally to dissolve the sugar. Partially cover, and cook until the quince is tender (about 45–60 minutes). Remove the lid and cook for a further 10–15 minutes until setting point is reached. Remove from heat, pour into warm, sterilised jars and seal.

Lemon and cranberry marmalade

Makes 6 × 190 g jars

450 g lemons, halved then
  thinly sliced

boiling water

5 cups white granulated sugar

1 cup frozen cranberries
  (defrosted)

Place lemons in a preserving pan and pour over enough boiling water to cover. Leave to stand overnight.

Drain the lemons, reserving the liquid. Remove the pips and tie in muslin. Return the lemons and pips to the preserving pan. Measure the soaking liquid and add fresh water to make about 5 cups. Place over a low heat and slowly bring to the boil. Simmer until tender (about 1 hour). Remove the muslin bag, first squeezing out any juice. Add the sugar and slowly bring to the boil, stirring occasionally until the sugar has dissolved. Cook for about 30 minutes until setting point is reached. Stir in the cranberries and cook over a low heat for a further 15–20 minutes. Remove from heat, pour into warm, sterilised jars and seal.

Seville orange marmalade

Seville oranges are in season for a short time during the winter. Take advantage of them as they do make the best orange marmalade

Makes approximately 12 × 375 g jars

1.5 kg Seville oranges

2 lemons

3 litres water

3 kg white granulated sugar

Juice the oranges and lemons. Catch the pips in a sieve and tie in muslin. Chop the peel into squares or thin strips, depending on the texture you like. Place the peel and juice in a preserving pan and pour in the water. Add the pips and bring mixture to the boil. Simmer for 1½–2 hours until the peel is soft. Remove the pips from the mixture, first squeezing the bag to extract any pectin-rich juice. Add the sugar and stir over a low heat until the sugar has dissolved. Boil for 20–30 minutes until setting point is reached. Cool a little to allow the peel to settle when bottled. Pour marmalade into warm, sterilised jars and seal.

Cumquat marmalade

Like Seville oranges, cumquats are in season for a short time and make one of the most flavoursome marmalades.

Makes approximately 5 × 375 g jars

1 kg cumquats
1 litre water

white granulated sugar
(for quantity see below)

Wash the fruit and slice thinly onto a plate to catch any juice and pips. Tie pips in a muslin bag and place in a bowl with the cumquats, juice and water. Leave overnight in a cool place.

Pour into a preserving pan and gently bring to the boil. Cook for about 1 hour, then remove from heat, cool and leave overnight.

Remove the pips from the mixture, squeezing the bag hard to extract any juice. Measure the liquid and cumquat pulp in a measuring jug and add the same amount of sugar. Place in a preserving pan and slowly bring to the boil, stirring to dissolve the sugar. Cook at a rapid boil until setting point is reached. Remove from heat, pour into warm, sterilised jars and seal.

Clear citrus marmalade

This marmalade is a good way to make the best of seasonal citrus fruit.

Makes approximately 4 × 500 g jars

1 kg citrus fruit (limes, mandarins, tangelos, pink grapefruit, oranges and lemons)

4 cups water (approx)

4 cups white granulated sugar (approx)

Remove the zest from all the fruit and shred finely. Squeeze the juice from the fruit and set aside. Collect the pips, finely chop the pith and tie both in a muslin bag. Soak the zest and the bag of pith and pips overnight in about 3 cups of water.

Place the soaked ingredients in a preserving pan with the soaking liquid. Add another cup of water, bring to the boil and cook until the zest is soft. Remove the muslin bag, first squeezing out any juice. Combine the juice from the fruit and zest and measure the amount. Add the same quantity of sugar. Return to the preserving pan and cook over a low heat until the sugar has dissolved, stirring occasionally. Bring to the boil and cook until setting point is reached. Remove from heat, pour into warm, sterilised jars and seal.

Pink grapefruit marmalade

Makes approximately 6 × 500 g jars

800 g pink grapefruit
250 g lemons

2 litres of water
2 kg white granulated sugar

Remove the zest from the grapefruit and slice thinly, then squeeze out the juice. Cut the lemons in half and squeeze out the juice. Remove lemon pips and tie in a muslin bag. Place grapefruit juice and zest, lemon juice and pips, and water in a bowl and soak overnight.

Place soaked ingredients and their liquid in a preserving pan and cook until the zest is soft. Remove the pips and add the sugar, dissolving it over a gentle heat. Bring to the boil and cook until setting point is reached. Remove from heat, pour into warm, sterilised jars and seal.

Pineapple citrus marmalade

Makes approximately 8 × 400 g jars

480 g peeled pineapple,
    cut into small chunks

480 g citrus fruit (lemon,
    lime, orange or tangelo)

3.5 litres water

1.5 kg white granulated sugar

4–5 tablespoons dark rum
    (optional)

Cut the citrus fruit in half and squeeze the juice. Keep the pips and tie them in muslin. Finely chop all the pith and peel, and place in a preserving pan with the chopped pineapple and the citrus pips. Pour in the water and slowly bring mixture to the boil. Simmer until tender (about 1 hour). Remove the bag of pips, first squeezing out any juice. Measure the pulp (approximately 1.75 litres) and return to the preserving pan. Add 500 g of sugar for every 600 ml of pulp (approximately 1.5 kg). Add the citrus juice, then slowly bring mixture to the boil. Cook until setting point is reached, then stir in the dark rum. Remove from heat, pour into warm, sterilised jars and seal.

Rhubarb marmalade

This is not a thick, sticky marmalade but more like
a preserve. It is not too sweet and spreads perfectly
on breakfast muffins or scones.

Makes approximately 5 × 350 g jars

2 oranges

2 lemons

1 litre water

700 g rhubarb, washed, trimmed
and cut into small chunks

5 g citric acid

700 g white granulated sugar

Remove the rind from the citrus fruits and squeeze the juice. Collect all
the pips. Blend the citrus pulp in a food processor, add to the pips and
tie in a muslin bag. Cut the rind into thin strips and place in a stainless
steel bowl with the juice, 500 ml of the water and the muslin bag.
Allow to stand overnight.

Transfer the citrus mixture to a preserving pan. Bring to the boil
and simmer until the rind is tender (50–60 minutes). Add the rhubarb,
citric acid and remaining 500 ml of water. Cook gently until the mixture
becomes thick and pulpy. Remove the bag, pressing it to extract any
juice. Stir in the sugar and bring to the boil. Cook until thick and set.
Remove from heat, pour into warm, sterilised jars and seal.

Tangerine marmalade

This is a lovely marmalade that again takes advantage
of a delicious winter citrus.

Makes approximately 6 × 210 g jars

950 g tangerines

1.75 litres water

1 kg white granulated sugar

200 ml lemon juice

Remove the peel from the tangerines, and shred. Cut the fruit in half
and squeeze out the juice, reserving the pips. Chop the pulp in a food
processor and tie in a muslin bag with the pips. Place the juice, muslin
bag, peel and water in a bowl and soak overnight.

Transfer soaked ingredients and liquid to a preserving pan and
bring to the boil. Simmer until the peel is tender (50–60 minutes).
Remove the muslin bag, first squeezing out any juice. Add the sugar
and lemon juice, and stir over a low heat until the sugar has dissolved.
Bring to the boil and cook until setting point is reached. Remove from
heat, pour into warm, sterilised jars and seal.

Kiwi fruit marmalade

Makes approximately 6 × 420 g jars

2 large oranges
1 large lemon
1 litre water

1 kg kiwi fruit
1 kg white granulated sugar

Remove the rind from the citrus fruit and squeeze the juice. Collect all the pips. Blend the citrus pulp in a food processor, add to the pips and tie in a muslin bag. Cut the rind into thin strips and place in a stainless steel bowl with the juice, water and pips. Allow to soak overnight.

Place the soaked ingredients in a preserving pan with their liquid. Bring to the boil and simmer until the peel is tender (about 50–60 minutes). Remove the muslin bag, first squeezing out any juice. Cut the kiwi fruit in half and scoop out the flesh with a spoon. Finely chop the flesh and add to the pan, cooking for a further 10–15 minutes until pulpy. Add the sugar and stir over a low heat until dissolved. Bring to the boil and cook until setting point is reached. Remove from heat, pour into warm, sterilised jars and seal.

Lime and ginger marmalade

Makes approximately 6 × 275 g jars

6 large limes, washed and thinly
   sliced, pips reserved

juice of 1 lemon, pips reserved

6 cups water

600 g white granulated sugar

3 tablespoons finely chopped,
   preserved ginger

Tie the lime and lemon pips in a muslin bag. Place in a bowl with
the sliced limes, lemon juice and water. Allow to stand overnight.

Transfer to a preserving pan and heat gently to boiling. Simmer
for 2 hours or until the lime peel is tender. (It is important to cook
the limes until the peel is soft. If the sugar is added and the peel is
not sufficiently cooked, the skin will toughen.) Remove the muslin
bag, first squeezing out any juice. Pour in an extra cup of water and
stir in the sugar and ginger. Dissolve the sugar over a gentle heat,
then bring mixture to the boil and cook until setting point is reached.
Remove from heat and cool a little before pouring into sterilised jars
and sealing.

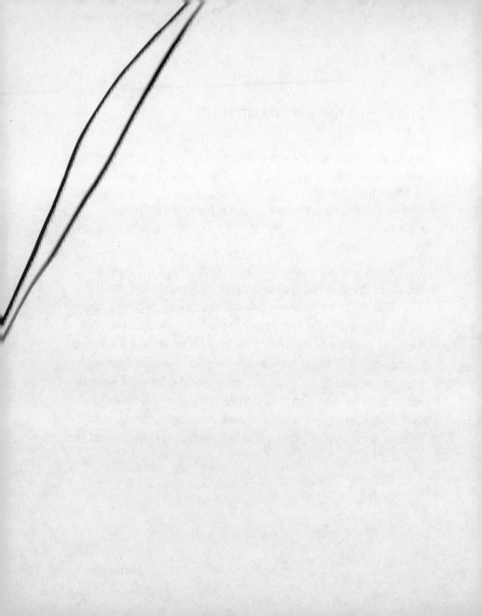

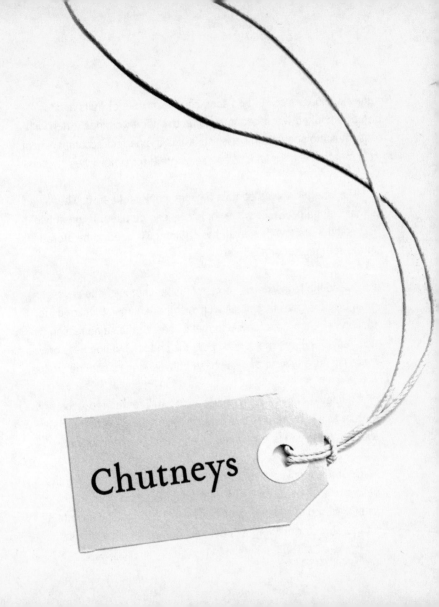

Chutneys

Chutney is usually a sweet and sour, chunky mixture of fruits and/or vegetables cooked with vinegar, sugar and other flavourings (often with chillies, mustard seeds or other spices). It is the perfect accompaniment to cold meats and grills and, of course, is great for sandwiches.

o   The vinegar should contain 5–6 per cent acetic acid. The sugar can be brown or white, or honey can be used. If these two ingredients are low, however, the chutney will need to be stored in the refrigerator or sterilised.

o   Due to the high vinegar content of most chutneys, the saucepan must be either stainless steel, aluminium, or enamel. Plastic lids for preserving jars are preferable to metal ones for the same reason (the acid reacts with the metal and spoils the chutney). If you have only metal lids, use a circle of cellophane between the lid and the chutney.

o   Chutney is cooked in an open pan to allow for the reduction of the mixture to a thick, jammy consistency. Stirring to prevent the chutney sticking to the pan is important in the latter stages of cooking.

o   Chutney should be kept in a cool dark place for 1–2 months before use, to allow the flavours to mature. Once opened, it is usually stored in the cupboard. However, if the recipe says to refrigerate after making, it is best consumed within a month.

Sicilian vegetable chutney

Makes approximately 5 × 250 g jars

½ cup virgin olive oil

1 large eggplant (500 g),
  cut into 2 cm pieces

1 red onion, chopped

1 red and 1 yellow capsicum,
  each chopped into 2 cm pieces

2 sticks celery, chopped

400 g ripe roma tomatoes,
  peeled, deseeded and chopped

2 cloves garlic, chopped

2 tablespoons red wine vinegar

1 teaspoon white granulated sugar

⅓ cup black kalamata olives, pitted

1 tablespoon salt-packed capers,
  rinsed

2 tablespoons currants

¼ cup chopped flat-leaf parsley

Heat ¼ cup of the oil in a large frying pan. Add eggplant and
cook over a high heat until browned. Remove from pan. Add another
2 tablespoons of olive oil to pan and cook onion, capsicum and celery
over medium heat until onion is soft.

Add tomatoes, garlic, vinegar and sugar, season to taste and
cook over a medium heat until tomatoes are reduced and pulpy (about
10 minutes). Stir in eggplant, olives, capers and currants, and simmer
another 5 minutes. Remove from heat, pour into warm, sterilised jars
and seal. Store in the refrigerator, or place in a water bath and process
for 30 minutes (see pages 9–10).

Pineapple mustard chutney

A lovely chutney to serve with barbecued pork sausages or chops.

Makes approximately 4 × 250 g jars

2 kg pineapple, peeled and cut into chunks

1 onion, finely chopped

1½ cups lime juice

1½ cups orange juice

grated rind of 2 limes

2 cups cider vinegar

3 cups white granulated sugar

1 teaspoon ground nutmeg

1 teaspoon ground cinnamon

1 cup raisins

1 tablespoon yellow mustard seeds

Place all the ingredients in a preserving pan and slowly bring to the boil over a gentle heat. Simmer, stirring occasionally, for 1–1½ hours until the mixture is sticky and thick. Remove from heat, pour into warm, sterilised jars and seal.

Fig, cumquat and rum chutney

This chutney is a delicious accompaniment to duck or
venison sausages. It also works well with aged cheddar.

Makes approximately 3 × 400 g jars

15 ripe cumquats, halved
and pips reserved

500 g Granny Smith apples,
cored and chopped

1 tablespoon ground ginger

225 ml cider vinegar

175 g golden syrup

1 onion, peeled and chopped

100 g dried figs, chopped

2 tablespoons raisins

1 tablespoon brown mustard seeds

1 teaspoon ground cardamom

500 ml water (approx)

¼ cup dark rum

¼ cup dark brown sugar

Finely chop the cumquats in a food processor and place in a bowl. Tie
the pips in a muslin bag and add to the bowl with the apples, ginger,
cider vinegar, golden syrup, onion, figs, raisins, mustard seeds and
cardamom. Pour over water to cover, and allow to stand overnight.

Place soaked ingredients and their liquid in a preserving pan and
cook until thick and pulpy (about 1 hour). Remove bag and squeeze
out any juice. Add the rum and brown sugar and stir over a low heat
until the sugar has dissolved. Cook for a further 15–20 minutes until
thick. Remove from heat, pour into warm, sterilised jars and seal.

Caramelised onion chutney

This is perfect for spreading on the base of a savoury tart or pizza. Use in a toasted sandwich with goat's cheese. It has so many uses that the tears caused by the onions are worth the trouble!

Makes approximately 6 × 450 g jars

¾ cup extra-virgin olive oil

3 kg onions, peeled and thinly sliced

1 cup dark brown sugar

500 ml balsamic vinegar

2 teaspoons fresh thyme leaves

1 teaspoon sea salt

Heat the oil in a preserving pan and add the onions. Stir for a couple of minutes, then cover and cook for about 40 minutes over a medium heat, stirring from time to time. Cook for a further 30 minutes uncovered, stirring occasionally. Stir in the sugar and balsamic vinegar, and bring to the boil. Turn down the heat and simmer for a further 30 minutes. Stir in the thyme leaves and salt, and cook for a further 10 minutes. The mixture should be thick and glossy. Remove from the heat, spoon into warm, sterilised jars and seal.

Autumn plum and peach chutney

Makes approximately 4 × 250 g jars

600 g peaches

600 g plums

2 red onions, peeled and chopped

1 whole lemon (peel finely
  chopped, pips removed and
  tied in a muslin bag)

1 tablespoon grated fresh ginger

½ cup cider vinegar

200 g white granulated sugar

1 tablespoon fresh sage leaves,
  chopped

Preheat oven to 200°C.

Plunge the peaches into boiling water for 4–5 minutes, then
remove the skins. Remove the stones from the fruit and roughly chop
the flesh. Place the peaches, plums, onions, lemon peel, ginger and
vinegar in a roasting tin and bake for 1 hour, tossing a few times
during the cooking.

Transfer roasted ingredients to a preserving pan and stir in the
sugar and reserved lemon pips. Stir until sugar has dissolved, bring
to the boil and cook at a low simmer for 30 minutes until thick and
syrupy. Remove pip bag. Stir in the sage leaves and cook for another
3–4 minutes.

Remove from heat, pour into warm, sterilised jars and seal.

Green tomato chutney

This is late-autumn chutney, when tomatoes are slow to ripen, and is a good, everyday condiment for sandwiches and cold meats.

Makes approximately 6 × 425 g jars

800 g green tomatoes

800 g apples, peeled and chopped

2 cloves garlic, peeled

2 teaspoons grated fresh ginger

300 g sultanas

500 g dark brown sugar

2 teaspoons allspice berries

2 teaspoon brown mustard seeds

700 ml white wine vinegar

Plunge the tomatoes into boiling water for 4–5 minutes, then remove the skins. Puree the tomatoes, apples, garlic and ginger in a food processor. Transfer to a preserving pan with the sugar and spices and cook for 1½ hours over a gentle heat until syrupy. Add the vinegar and cook for a further 40 minutes until reduced, thick and syrupy. Remove from heat, pour into warm, sterilised jars and seal.

Roasted corn relish

Here the vegetables are cooked first and then a flavoured,
sweetened vinegar is added.

Makes approximately 6 × 300 g jars

1 red capsicum, deseeded and
finely chopped

1 green capsicum, deseeded and
finely chopped

1 large onion, finely chopped

2 cloves garlic, chopped

1 long red chilli, deseeded and
chopped

3 corn cobs, kernels removed

½ cup virgin olive oil

3 cups red wine vinegar

1½ cups white granulated sugar

2 teaspoons yellow mustard seeds

2 teaspoon turmeric

Preheat oven to 180°C.

Mix the prepared vegetables together in a baking dish and
stir the oil through. Roast for about 1 hour, then remove and allow
to cool slightly.

In a saucepan combine the vinegar, sugar, mustard seeds and
turmeric. Bring to the boil, stirring to dissolve the sugar. Boil for
10 minutes to reduce a little. Spoon the vegetables into sterilised
preserving jars, then pour in the vinegar mixture. Pour a little oil
over the top to cover, and seal.

Cranberry and orange relish

This all-time Christmas favourite is lovely with ham and turkey, but you can also use it during the year with roast pork or barbecued sausages, or in ham or turkey sandwiches.

Makes approximately 10 × 350 g jars

2 kg frozen cranberries

1.75 kg white granulated sugar

2 tablespoons balsamic vinegar

8 oranges

500 ml freshly squeezed orange juice

Defrost the cranberries and place in a preserving pan with the sugar and balsamic vinegar. Remove the zest from the oranges, squeeze the juice and remove the pips. Finely chop the flesh in a food processor and add to the pan with the zest. Measure the juice and make it up to 1 litre with extra freshly squeezed orange juice. Slowly bring to the boil, stirring from time to time. Boil for approximately 45–50 minutes until thick and jammy. Remove from heat, pour into warm, sterilised jars and seal.

Indian-style eggplant chutney

Makes approximately 4 × 350 g jars

1.5 kg firm eggplants, cubed

1 tablespoon salt

1 tablespoon ground turmeric

1 tablespoon brown mustard seeds

1 cup white wine vinegar

2 cloves garlic, peeled

1 large red onion, peeled
  and quartered

2 green chillies

½ cup vegetable oil

1 tablespoon ground cumin

1 tablespoon ground coriander

1 tablespoon fennel seeds

1 cinnamon stick

400 ml water

2 tablespoons tamarind paste

2 tablespoons brown sugar

Mix the eggplant with the salt and turmeric. Cover and allow to stand overnight.

Drain and rinse the eggplant and pat dry. Blend the mustard seeds, vinegar, garlic, onion and chillies to a paste. Heat the oil in a preserving pan and fry the eggplant in batches for 3–4 minutes, adding more oil if necessary. Remove and set aside. Stir in the vinegar paste and add the cumin, coriander, fennel and cinnamon. Cook for 2–3 minutes, then add the water and tamarind paste and bring to the boil. Add the eggplant, cook for 2–3 minutes, then bring to the boil and add the sugar. Cook for 20 minutes until reduced. Pour into warm, sterilised jars and seal.

Roasted beetroot and orange chutney

Makes approximately 6 × 180 g jars

880 g beetroot, trimmed
and washed

zest of 1 orange

150 ml white wine vinegar

150 g white granulated sugar

1 cinnamon stick

1 medium red onion,
peeled and finely chopped

Preheat oven to 200°C.

Wrap the beetroot in foil and bake for 1 hour, or until tender. Remove and cool a little before peeling. Grate the cooked beetroot.

Finely chop the orange zest and place it in a saucepan with the vinegar, sugar, cinnamon stick and onion and bring slowly to the boil. Cook for 5 minutes, then add the grated beetroot and cook for 10 minutes until reduced. Remove from heat, pour into warm, sterilised jars and seal.

Sterilise in a hot-water bath for 30 minutes (see pages 9–10), or store in the refrigerator.

Pear chutney with craisins

Craisins are sweetened, dried cranberries and can be used when fresh or frozen cranberries aren't available. They are great to add to chutneys instead of raisins or sultanas.

Makes approximately 4 × 300 g jars

1 kg pears, peeled, cored and finely chopped

2 red onions, finely chopped

1 tablespoon finely chopped fresh ginger

2 cloves garlic, chopped

1 red chilli, chopped

1 cup red wine vinegar

200 g brown sugar

3 tablespoons dried craisins

Preheat oven to 180°C.

Place all the ingredients in a shallow baking dish and mix well. Cook for 30 minutes. Turn up the oven to 200°C and cook for a further 20–30 minutes. Remove from the oven, spoon into warm, sterilised jars and seal.

Pineapple and chilli chutney

Makes approximately 5 × 320 g jars

700 g pineapple, peeled and
  coarsely chopped

500 g roma tomatoes,
  peeled and chopped

3 long green chillies, chopped

1 cup brown sugar

3 cups white wine vinegar

1 teaspoon salt

Place all the ingredients in a preserving pan and slowly bring to the
boil, stirring occasionally. Simmer for 20 minutes. Remove from heat
and blend or process. Return to the pan and cook for a further
10 minutes. Remove from heat, pour into warm, sterilised jars
and seal.

Beetroot and apple chutney

Makes approximately 6 × 250 g jars

750 g beetroot, peeled and grated

500 g apples, peeled, cored and
    chopped

1 onion, chopped

750 ml malt vinegar

500 g white granulated sugar

1 tablespoon grated fresh ginger

200 g raisins

Place all the ingredients in a preserving pan and leave to stand
for 2 hours.

Place pan over a medium heat and slowly bring contents to the
boil. Simmer for 1½–2 hours until reduced, thick and syrupy. Remove
from heat, pour into warm, sterilised jars and seal.

Red capsicum and tomato chutney

Makes approximately 4 × 380 g jars

450 g tomatoes

1 kg red capsicum, deseeded and chopped

250 g red onion, chopped

2 cloves garlic, chopped

2 red chillies, deseeded and chopped

10 allspice berries

100 ml olive oil

300 g white granulated sugar

150 g sultanas

250 ml white wine vinegar

Preheat oven to 175°C.

Plunge tomatoes into boiling water for 4 minutes, then remove the skins. Chop roughly and place in a baking dish with the capsicum, onion, garlic, chillies, allspice and olive oil. Cook for 1 hour in the oven, stirring occasionally. Turn up the heat to 200°C and stir in the sugar, sultanas and vinegar. Mix well and cook for a further hour to reduce the liquid, stirring occasionally. Remove from heat, pour into warm, sterilised jars and seal.

Hot fried chilli chutney

This classic, Indonesian-style sambal is a great accompaniment to grilled spicy meats or fish.

Makes approximately 4 × 200 g jars

250 ml peanut oil

12 long red chillies, roughly chopped

4 onions, chopped

1 head of garlic, peeled and crushed

12 macadamia nuts, chopped

2 tablespoons dark brown sugar or dark palm sugar

2 tablespoons rice vinegar

2 stalks lemongrass (white part only) roughly chopped

4 tablespoons coconut cream

Combine the oil, chillies, onion and garlic in a food processor or blender and process to a rough paste.

Place a heavy-based frying pan over a low heat. Add the paste and cook for 10 minutes. Stir in the nuts, sugar, vinegar, lemongrass and coconut cream. Cook over a low heat until most of the liquid has evaporated and the mixture has thickened. Remove from heat and pour into warm, sterilised jars. Pour a little chilli oil (see page 122) over the top, then seal.

Store in the refrigerator.

Mango chutney

Makes approximately 6 × 220 g jars

4 cloves

10 black peppercorns

½ teaspoon allspice berries

2 red onions, roughly chopped

400 ml malt vinegar

2 bay leaves

1 fresh red chilli, sliced

1 kg firm mangoes, peeled, stoned and cut into wedges

350 g green apples, peeled, cored and sliced

1 teaspoon black mustard seeds, dry-toasted in a hot pan till they pop

450 g white granulated sugar

1 teaspoon ground ginger

Tie the cloves, peppercorns and allspice berries in a muslin bag. Place in a preserving pan with the onions, vinegar, bay leaves and chilli and simmer until the onions are tender. Add the mangoes, apples and mustard seeds, and cook for about 15 minutes until the fruit is soft. Dissolve the sugar and ground ginger over a low heat. Bring to the boil and cook until thick and syrupy, stirring occasionally. Remove from heat, pour into warm, sterilised jars and seal.

Papaya, chilli and ginger chutney

Makes approximately 5 × 275 g jars

1 litre cider vinegar

1 tablespoon tamarind paste

2 teaspoons allspice berries

1 whole star anise

1 kg red papaya, peeled and roughly chopped

1 red capsicum, deseeded and roughly chopped

6 cloves garlic, chopped

3 large red onions, roughly chopped

3 chillies, deseeded and chopped

1 stalk lemongrass (white part only) bruised and chopped

4 tablespoons grated fresh ginger

600 g soft brown sugar

Place the vinegar and spices in a preserving pan and bring to the boil. Simmer for 5 minutes. Add all the other ingredients and slowly return to the boil. Lower the heat and simmer for 30 minutes, stirring occasionally to prevent sticking.

Remove from heat and take out the star anise and allspice. Spoon chutney into warm, sterilised jars and seal.

Like chutneys, pickles are a combination of fruits or vegetables preserved in a solution of vinegar, spices and sometimes a little sugar. They are an excellent accompaniment to cold meats and fish, as well adding flavour to salads and sandwiches. The vegetables normally have a crunchy texture and can make an interesting addition to an antipasto platter, or served with drinks before a meal.

- Vinegar chosen for pickling should contain at least 5–6 per cent acetic acid.

- Salt is used in some recipes to draw out water or bitterness from the vegetable – this maximises the vinegar's strength. Sea salt is the best to use for this purpose.

- Pickles should be stored in a dark, cool cupboard for at least 1 month before using.

Spiced pickled sweet plums

Makes approximately 2 × 500 g jars

1 kg small, firm plums

1 teaspoon whole cloves

4 star anise

6 cardamom pods

1 cinnamon stick

1 kg brown sugar

1 litre red wine vinegar

Prick the skins of the plums and set aside.

Place the remaining ingredients in a preserving pan and cook over a medium heat, stirring to dissolve the sugar. Bring to the boil and cook until reduced a little (about 10 minutes). Add the plums and cook for 10–15 minutes until tender. Remove plums and spices, and pack into warm sterilised jars. Pour the vinegar syrup over, and seal.

Spiced Indian-style onion pickle

This sweet pickle is lovely served with spicy grilled meats or fish.

Makes approximately 3 × 485 g jars

1 tablespoon sea salt

1 kg red onions, peeled and cut into eighths

200 ml vegetable oil

1½ tablespoons brown mustard seeds

1 teaspoon freshly grated turmeric (or ½ teaspoon ground)

100 ml malt vinegar

100 g dark brown sugar

2 cloves garlic, sliced

3 long red or green chillies, deseeded and sliced

2 teaspoons freshly grated ginger

juice and grated zest of 1 lime

Sprinkle salt over the onions. Set aside for 2 hours to sweat and soften. Drain and rinse well.

Heat the oil in a preserving pan. Add the mustard seeds and cook until they pop. Stir in the turmeric, vinegar and sugar and bring to the boil. Stir in the drained onions, the garlic, chillies and ginger. Cook over a medium heat until the onions are soft (about 15–20 minutes). Stir in the lime juice and zest and cook for a further 10 minutes until syrupy. Remove from heat and pour into warm sterilised jars. Cover the top with a little oil before sealing.

Roasted red onions in balsamic vinegar with thyme sprigs

Makes approximately 4 × 250 g jars

1 kg small red onions
1 cup dark balsamic vinegar
1 cup white balsamic vinegar

160 g white granulated sugar
4–5 thyme sprigs

Preheat oven to 180°C.

Place the whole onions in a baking tin and roast for 1–2 hours until soft. Remove from the oven and cover with a tea-towel for 10 minutes. Peel off the skins and cut the onions into quarters.

In a saucepan dissolve the sugar in the vinegar and bring to the boil. Boil for 10 minutes to reduce. Pack the onions into warm, sterilised jars with a few thyme sprigs and pour the vinegar syrup over. Seal and store in a cool dark place for 3 months before using. Refrigerate after opening.

Pickled fennel

Serve this pickle with grilled or smoked fish.

Makes approximately 3 × 330 g jars

3 litres salted water

1 kg fresh fennel bulbs, trimmed and very thinly sliced

1 tablespoon peppercorns

1 litre white wine vinegar

grated rind of 1 lemon

¼ cup white granulated sugar

fennel leaves

virgin olive oil

Bring the salted water to the boil and blanch the fennel. Remove, drain and refresh under cold water. Drain again. Place the peppercorns, vinegar, lemon rind and sugar in a saucepan and bring to the boil. Cook for 10 minutes to reduce. Place the drained fennel into sterilised jars with a few fennel leaves and pour the vinegar syrup over. Top with a little oil and seal.

Spiced pickled cumquats

This is the perfect pickle to serve with duck or venison.

Makes approximately 6 × 300 g jars

1 stick cinnamon

6 allspice berries

2 teaspoons black peppercorns

500 ml white wine vinegar

500 ml water

500 g white granulated sugar

800 g cumquats, halved and pips removed

6 bay leaves

Combine the cinnamon, allspice, peppercorns, vinegar, water and sugar in a saucepan and cook over a gentle heat until the sugar has dissolved. Add cumquats, bring to the boil and cook for a further 10 minutes. Remove from heat and pour into warm, sterilised jars. Place a bay leaf in each jar before sealing.

Leave in a dark cupboard for 4–5 weeks. Refrigerate after opening.

Roasted red and yellow capsicum with chilli pickle

Makes approximately 2 × 500 g jars

750 g red capsicum

750 g yellow capsicum

50 g chillies (long red and green)

150 ml extra-virgin olive oil

salt and ground black pepper

800 ml white wine vinegar

1 tablespoon balsamic vinegar

80 g brown sugar

2 cloves garlic, peeled and sliced

6 bay leaves

Preheat oven to 200°C.

Deseed capsicums and chillies and cut into strips. Place in a roasting tin with the oil and season with salt and pepper. Roast the capsicum and chillies until soft (30–50 minutes).

Meanwhile place the vinegars, sugar, garlic and bay leaves in a saucepan and slowly bring to the boil to dissolve the sugar. Boil for 10 minutes to reduce a little.

Place the capsicum and chillies in warm, sterilised preserving jars. Pour the hot vinegar syrup over and seal. Store pickle for 2 months in a cool, dark cupboard to mature before using. Refrigerate after opening.

Pickled Indian limes

Makes approximately 3 × 400 g jars

20 small limes, cut into quarters

1 cup sea salt

juice of 5 limes

3 tablespoons vegetable oil

1 tablespoon brown mustard seeds

1 tablespoon fenugreek seeds

1 cinnamon stick

2 teaspoons ground turmeric

2 green chillies, cut into thin strips

1–2 sprigs fresh curry leaves
  (or dried)

extra lime juice (4–5 limes)

chilli oil (see page 122)

Mix the limes and sea salt in a bowl. Pack salted limes into a sterilised jar and top with the freshly squeezed lime juice. Seal and leave for a week in a warm, sunny spot.

Heat the oil in a frying pan and fry the spices for 2–3 minutes. Transfer the limes to smaller, sterilised jars. Stir in the fried spices, chilli and curry leaves. Top with more lime juice to cover and pour a little chilli oil over the top before sealing.

Store for 2 months before using.

Pickled chargrilled orange, red and green chillies

Serve these colourful, spicy chillies as an antipasto; the larger chillies are usually not as hot as the smaller ones.

Makes approximately 2 × 750 g jars

500 g long red, green and orange chillies, washed

5 cups white wine vinegar

¾ cup brown sugar

1 teaspoon salt

1 teaspoon coriander seeds

1 teaspoon allspice berries

1 teaspoon black peppercorns

1 teaspoon cumin seeds

Heat a chargrill pan to high and cook the chillies each side to char the skins a little (about 2–3 minutes). (If you don't have a chargrill pan, roast in a hot oven (200°C) for 10–15 minutes until the skins are blistered.) In a saucepan heat the vinegar, sugar and spices over a low heat until the sugar is dissolved. Bring to the boil and cook for 5 minutes. Remove from heat. Place the chillies in warm, sterilised jars and pour the hot vinegar mixture over. Seal and store in a cool, dark cupboard for 4–5 weeks before using.

Pumpkin and ginger pickle

This unusual pickle can be served on an antipasto plate or eaten on its own with drinks – it goes well with a dry sherry.

Makes approximately 4 × 300 g jars

800 g peeled pumpkin, cut into small cubes

50 g sea salt

500 ml white wine vinegar

500 ml white wine

1 teaspoon black peppercorns

¼ teaspoon chilli flakes

750 g dark brown sugar

200 g crystallised ginger

4 bay leaves

Place the pumpkin in a bowl and stir in the salt. Leave overnight weighted down with a plate to help squeeze out the moisture.

Combine the vinegar, wine, spices and sugar in a preserving pan and heat over a low heat until the sugar is dissolved. Bring to the boil and simmer for 5 minutes.

Rinse the pumpkin. Chop the ginger into small pieces and mix with the pumpkin. Spoon pumpkin and ginger into warm, sterilised jars. Pour the vinegar over, add the bay leaves and seal. Store for 2 months before opening.

Pickled chargrilled Japanese eggplant with mint

Makes approximately 3 × 250 g jars

700 g small Japanese eggplants, trimmed, halved lengthways then quartered

⅓ cup olive oil

⅓ cup balsamic vinegar

4 cloves garlic, peeled and cut into slivers

½ teaspoon finely chopped fresh mint

Preheat a grill pan or barbecue grill and cook the eggplant both sides until soft and charred. Transfer to a bowl and cover with a tea-towel.

Whisk the oil and vinegar together and stir in the garlic and mint. Pour over the chargrilled eggplant. Place in sterilised jars, top up with extra olive oil to cover, and seal. Store in a cool dark place for 3 weeks. Refrigerate once opened.

Sweet chilli beetroot pickle

Makes approximately 5 × 300 g jars

1.2 kg beetroot, trimmed
and washed

500 g sugar

250 ml red wine vinegar

1 red chilli, finely chopped

Preheat oven to 180°C.

Wrap beetroot in foil, place on a baking tray and cook until tender (about 40 minutes). Remove and cool a little before peeling.

Place the sugar, vinegar and chilli in a preserving pan and heat gently to dissolve the sugar. Chop the beetroot into small chunks and add to the pan. Cook for 40–50 minutes until the beetroot is glossy and sticky. Remove from heat, spoon into warm, sterilised jars and seal.

Store in the fridge after opening.

Garden harvest pickled vegetables

Makes 1 large jar (approximately 1.25 litres)

2 cups water

2 cups cider vinegar

2 cups rice vinegar

2 cups sugar

1 tablespoon salt

2 tablespoons coriander seeds

2 cinnamon sticks

3 whole cloves

5 allspice berries

3 whole bay leaves

4 sprigs fresh thyme

4 sprigs fresh marjoram

8 small pickling onions, peeled and quartered

1 whole head of garlic, peeled

2 carrots, peeled and cut into rounds

2 red capsicum, deseeded and cut into strips

1 yellow capsicum, deseeded and cut into strips

1 green capsicum deseeded and cut into strips

4 jalapeño chillies, sliced into rings

6 serrano chillies, sliced into rings

Place the first 12 ingredients in a preserving pan and slowly bring to the boil. Add the onions, garlic and carrots, return to the boil and cook for about 5 minutes. Add the capsicum and chillies and cook a further 2 minutes, being careful not to overcook the vegetables. Remove from heat, pour into warm, sterilised jars and seal.

Store pickle for 1 month before using. Refrigerate after opening.

Spiced pickled pears

Makes approximately 4 × 500 g jars

500 ml white wine vinegar

500 g brown sugar

1 teaspoon ground cloves

1 stick cinnamon

2 teaspoons juniper berries

1 small red chilli, deseeded
and cut into strips

1 kg pears, peeled, cored
and quartered

Place the vinegar, sugar, spices and chilli in a preserving pan. Cook
over a medium heat to dissolve the sugar. Add pears to the vinegar
mixture. Bring to the boil and cook for 10–15 minutes until the pears
are tender. Remove from heat, pour into warm, sterilised jars and seal.

Pub-style pickled onions

Makes approximately 2 × 750 g jars

1 kg small pickling onions

¼ cup salt

600 ml water

3 cups malt vinegar

200 ml red wine vinegar

1 cup honey

1 teaspoon yellow mustard seeds

2 teaspoons black peppercorns

1 teaspoon allspice berries

1 teaspoon fennel seeds

Plunge the pickling onions into a bowl of boiling water and leave for 3–4 minutes. Remove the skins. Place onions in a sterilised glass preserving jar and cover with the sugar and water. Leave for 5 days in a cool dark place.

Heat the vinegar, honey and spices together until the honey is dissolved. Drain the onions and pack into sterilised jars, add enough pickling vinegar to cover completely, then seal.

Leave for 2–3 weeks to mature before opening.

Vinegars, sauces & syrups

Sauces and syrups are usually pureed fruits or vegetables used as condiments, or as bases for making or enhancing other sauces (for example, fruit syrup stirred through cream).

The method for producing ketchups and sauces is similar to that used for chutneys and, like chutney, if there is little sugar or vinegar in the recipe then ketchups can be sterilised to add storage life, or stored in the refrigerator for a short period.

Blackberry vinegar

This lively vinegar can be poured over summer fruits, or mixed with olive oil to make an interesting salad dressing for bitter leaves like radicchio or endive.

Makes approximately 4 × 175 ml bottles

450 g fresh blackberries

550 ml white wine vinegar

white granulated sugar (for quantity see below)

Place the blackberries and vinegar in a glass jar. Seal and leave in a sunny spot for 4 days.

Drain, setting blackberries aside. Measure the liquid and place in a preserving pan with 225 g of sugar for every 450 ml of liquid. Dissolve the sugar over a low heat. Bring to the boil and cook for 10 minutes. Mash the blackberries and strain into the pan. Cook for a further 5 minutes. Remove from heat, pour into warm, sterilised jars and seal.

Strawberry vinegar

Makes approximately 5 × 250 ml bottles

500 g strawberries, hulled

300 ml mirin (rice wine) vinegar

300 ml white wine vinegar

500 g white granulated sugar
(for quantity see below)

Place the strawberries and vinegars together in a glass jar and seal.
Place in a sunny spot for 4 days.

Mash the strawberries and vinegar and strain into a preserving
pan. Measure liquid and add 225 g sugar for every 600 ml. Cook
over a low heat to dissolve the sugar. Bring to the boil and cook for
10 minutes. Remove from heat, pour into warm, sterilised jars
and seal.

Tarragon vinegar

Sometimes hard to find in delicatessens, this vinegar makes a lovely dressing for seafood, eggs, and chicken salad.

Makes 1 × 500 ml bottle

10 tablespoons fresh tarragon
   leaves (use dried if unavailable)

2 cups white wine vinegar

fresh sprigs of tarragon

Place the tarragon leaves and vinegar in a glass preserving jar with a vinegar-proof lid. Leave in a warm sunny spot for a week, shaking the jar daily.

Strain vinegar through a fine plastic sieve. Transfer to a clean, sterilised jar with the fresh tarragon sprigs. Seal and store in a dark cupboard.

Roasted tomato ketchup

Makes approximately 4 × 225 ml bottles

600 g slow roasted tomatoes
(see page 119)

1 roasted red capsicum, skin and
seeds removed

salt and pepper to taste

2 bird's eye chillies

1 tablespoon red wine vinegar

1 tablespoon soft brown sugar

Place all the ingredients in a preserving pan and bring to the boil.
Blend to a puree. Simmer for 10 minutes. Remove from heat,
pour into warm, sterilised jars and seal.

Keep refrigerated, or process filled bottles in a water bath
for 30 minutes (see pages 9–10).

Mushroom ketchup

An English-style ketchup that goes well with a full, cooked breakfast. Or spread it on a bun with a grilled hamburger.

Makes approximately 3 × 250 ml jars

1 kg field mushrooms, sliced

1 tablespoon sea salt

300 ml malt vinegar

2 medium onions, chopped

1 clove garlic, chopped

2 tablespoons low-salt soy sauce

2 tablespoons brandy

Place mushrooms in a bowl and mix the salt through. Leave for 24 hours.

Combine the vinegar, onions and garlic in a preserving pan. Bring to the boil and simmer for 5 minutes. Add the mushrooms and any liquid formed in the bowl. Bring to the boil and simmer for 1 hour. Puree the mixture with a hand electric blender or in a food processor, then return to the boil. Add the soy sauce and brandy and simmer for 5 minutes. Remove from heat, pour into warm, sterilised jars and seal.

Alternatively, sterilise filled bottles in a water bath for 10 minutes (see pages 9–10). Tighten the caps once processed.

Porcini mushroom ketchup

Makes approximately 4 × 220 ml jars

750 g field mushrooms

1 tablespoon sea salt

15 g dried porcini mushrooms

15 g dried shiitake mushrooms

500 ml hot water

1 small onion, roughly chopped

2 cloves garlic, peeled

450 ml white wine vinegar

2 bay leaves

ground black pepper

½ teaspoon ground mace

¼ cup medium sherry

Wipe the field mushrooms clean, trim the stalks and slice. Place in a mixing bowl, stir in the sea salt and leave for 24 hours.

Soak the dried mushrooms in the hot water until soft.

Puree the salted mushrooms, onion and garlic in a food processor, then transfer to a preserving pan. Puree the soaked mushrooms and their liquid in the food processor, then add to the mushroom mixture in the pan. Add the vinegar and spices and bring to the boil. Simmer for 1 hour until the ketchup is thick. Remove the bay leaves and puree the ketchup again with a hand-held electric blender. Add the sherry and boil rapidly for a further 5 minutes. Remove from heat, pour into warm, sterilised jars and seal. Refrigerate after opening.

Papaya, capsicum and chilli ketchup

Makes approximately 5 × 225 ml jars

500 g red papaya, deseeded,
peeled and cut into chunks

1 large red capsicum, deseeded
and finely chopped

2 red chillies, deseeded and finely
chopped

2 cloves garlic, chopped

2 red onions, chopped

500 ml white vinegar

2 teaspoons Dijon mustard

4 tablespoons brown sugar

pinch of salt

Place all the ingredients in a preserving pan and slowly bring to the
boil. Cook for 30–40 minutes until the vegetables are very soft and
the liquid is reduced and smooth. Remove from heat, pour into warm,
sterilised jars and seal.

Store in the fridge after opening.

Fresh tomato sauce

Roma tomatoes are at their best in the summer. This sauce is easy to make and you can add your own special stamp with herbs, garlic, spices and wine.

Makes approximately 2 × 300 g jars

1 kg ripe roma tomatoes, washed and roughly chopped

150 ml red wine

3 tablespoons virgin olive oil

1 onion, finely chopped

2 cloves garlic, finely chopped

salt and pepper

In a saucepan cook the tomatoes, covered, over a medium heat for 15 minutes. Add the red wine and cook a further 15 minutes.

Meanwhile, heat the oil in a frying pan and cook the onion and garlic over a low heat until soft. Remove tomatoes from heat and blend to a puree. Push through a fine sieve to remove the skin and pips. Pour back into the saucepan and add the onion and garlic. Cook for 30 minutes until reduced. Season to taste with salt and pepper.

Remove from heat and pour into warm, sterilised jars leaving 2 cm at the top. Sterilise filled bottles in a water bath for 40 minutes (see pages 9–10).

Tomato sauce with whole, mini roma tomatoes and herbs

Makes approximately 2 × 300 g jars

1 kg roma tomatoes, washed
and roughly chopped

1 onion, chopped

2 bay leaves

2 sprigs thyme

2 sprigs oregano

juice of 1 lemon

salt and pepper to season

1 tablespoon balsamic vinegar

1 tablespoon sugar

450 g mini roma tomatoes, washed

Combine the chopped tomatoes and onion and herbs in a preserving pan. Cover and cook over a low heat for 15–20 minutes. Remove the herbs. Blend or puree the tomatoes, then sieve to remove the skin and pips. Return to the pan with the lemon juice, seasoning, vinegar and sugar. Simmer for 10 minutes.

Meanwhile cut the mini roma tomatoes in half and place them in warm, sterilised preserving jars. Ladle the tomato sauce into each jar and seal. Sterilise filled jars in a hot-water bath for 40 minutes (see pages 9–10).

Spicy, aromatic tomato sauce

Makes approximately 6 × 250 g jars

8 whole cloves

2 teaspoons whole
  cardamom pods

1 teaspoon black peppercorns

2 whole star anise

1 bay leaf

1 cinnamon stick

1.5 kg tomatoes

1 tablespoon olive oil

2 green chillies, deseeded
  and chopped

1 onion, chopped

2 cloves garlic, crushed

6 tablespoons dark brown sugar

1 tablespoon yellow mustard seeds

3 cups cider vinegar

juice and grated zest of 2 limes

1 teaspoon salt

Combine the spices and tie into a muslin bag. Score the skins of the
tomatoes then plunge into boiling water for 4–5 minutes. Remove
the skins.

Heat the oil in a preserving pan and cook the chillies, onion and
garlic over a low heat until soft. Stir in the peeled tomatoes, sugar,
mustard seeds, salt and spice bag. Bring to the boil and simmer for
1 hour until reduced and thickened. Add the vinegar, lime juice and
zest and cook for a further 30 minutes. Take out the spice bag.
Remove sauce from heat, pour into warm, sterilised jars and seal.

Store in a cool, dark cupboard.

Spicy plum sauce

Delicious served with grilled duck breast or barbecued
kebabs and pork ribs.

Makes approximately 4 × 280 ml bottles

1.5 kg plums, chopped
   and stones removed

1 large red onion, finely chopped

1 × 2 cm knob fresh ginger, grated

2 red chillies, deseeded
   and chopped

6 star anise

1 cup red wine vinegar

3 cups soft brown sugar

Place the plums, onion, ginger, chillies, star anise and vinegar in
a preserving pan. Slowly bring to the boil and simmer for 15 minutes
until the plums collapse. Add the brown sugar and cook, stirring until
the sugar has dissolved. Bring to the boil and cook for 20 minutes.
Remove from heat and sieve into another pan. Cook for a further
5 minutes. Remove from heat, pour into warm, sterilised bottles
and seal.

Pomegranate syrup

This syrup can be poured over ice cream or fruit salad, or added to champagne or mineral water.

Makes approximately 2 × 250 ml bottles

2–3 whole pomegranates, seeds removed

2½ cups sugar

½ cup water

Blend pomegranates in a food processor. Transfer to a glass jar with the sugar and water. Seal and leave in a sunny spot for 2 days.

Place pomegranate puree in a jelly bag and allow the juice to drip through for 2–3 hours. Transfer the juice to a preserving pan and slowly bring to the boil. Simmer for 2–3 minutes. Remove from heat, pour into warm, sterilised jars and seal.

Lemon liqueur (Limoncello)

A delicious alcoholic treat to pour over ice cream or gelato.
You can also place it in a tall glass with ice and top up
with soda.

Makes approximately 2 × 750 ml bottles

6 lemons

750 ml vodka

225 g caster sugar

450 ml water

Wash the lemons and use a vegetable peeler to carefully remove
the peel only – leave behind the pith. Place the peel strips in a glass
preserving jar, pour the vodka over and seal. Keep in a cool dark place
for 2 weeks.

In a saucepan, dissolve the sugar in the water and bring to the
boil. Cook for 5 minutes. Remove from heat and allow to completely
cool. Pour the sugar syrup into the vodka and lemon mixture and seal.
Leave for a further week.

Strain the mixture. Transfer to sterilised bottles and seal. Store
in a cool, dark cupboard until ready to use.

Other Preserves

This chapter contains delightful recipes for whole-produce preserves such as cured olives, asparagus in oil, cherries in brandy and preserved Moroccan lemons. There are also recipes for fruit curd and fruit cheese.

Fruit curds are rich in sugar, butter and eggs. They are lovely spread on scones and toast, or folded through whipped cream and used to fill cakes and tarts. Once cooled, and the jar sealed, they should be refrigerated.

Fruit cheese is a simpler recipe, usually fruit and sugar. The result is like a very stiff fruit jelly that can be cut into chunks or slices. It is excellent served with a cheese platter or with savoury dishes.

Slow-roasted tomatoes

There are so many uses for these tomatoes – in salads,
pizzas, sandwiches or antipasto platters, as well as in
ketchups and chutneys. You can add extra ingredients
like chopped fresh basil leaves or grated lemon rind when
packing the tomatoes into airtight containers. Some recipes
call for them to be packed in oil, but I find the juices and
cooking oil provide enough moisture. Use them up quickly
and make more – it is worth the effort.

Makes approximately 3.5 kg

5 kg roma tomatoes

20 cloves garlic, peeled and sliced

2 tablespoons sea salt

1 cup virgin olive oil

Preheat oven to 150°C.

Cut the tomatoes into quarters and place them skin-side down
on shallow baking trays. Sprinkle the sea salt and pour the oil over.
Distribute the slivers of garlic over the top. Bake in a fan-forced oven
for 2–3 hours (a little longer in a regular oven). Cool and pack into
airtight containers. Refrigerate for up to 3 weeks.

Cured green olives

Green olives are unripe and so quite bitter. It is important to remove the bitterness before curing them.

Makes approximately 2 × 500 g jars

1 kg green olives, pricked with a pin or skewer

boiling water

100 ml white wine vinegar

100 g salt

1 litre water

olive oil

Wash the olives and place in a sterilised glass preserving jar. Pour boiling water over. Fill a plastic bag with water, tie it at the top and place over the olives to keep them completely submerged and all air out. Leave for 24 hours.

Repeat this process for the next 4 days.

Make a brine comprising the vinegar, salt and water. Drain the olives, place in a sterilised glass jar and cover with the brine. Top with a little oil and seal. Store in a cool, dark cupboard for 1 month before opening.

For extra flavour add to the brine: 1 tablespoon fennel seeds, 2 bay leaves, 12 coriander seeds and 4 strips of lemon peel. Boil the brine and cool completely before pouring over the olives and sealing.

Cured black olives

Black olives are ripe, and do not need as much processing as the unripe fruit. Purple olives, however, need just as much processing as green ones.

Makes approximately 2 × 500 g jars

1 kg black olives, pricked
   with a pin or skewer

boiling water

100 ml white wine vinegar

100 g salt

1 litre water

olive oil

Wash the olives and place in a sterilised glass preserving jar. Pour over boiling water to cover. Fill a plastic bag with water, tie at the top and place over the olives to keep them completely submerged and all air out. Leave for 24 hours. Repeat this process for the next 2 days.

Make a brine comprising the vinegar, salt and water. Drain the olives and place in a sterilised glass jar. Pour in the brine to cover. Top with a little oil and seal. Store in a cool, dark cupboard for 10 days before opening.

For extra flavour add to the brine 1 teaspoon dried chilli flakes, 2 bay leaves, 4 strips orange peel and 1 teaspoon cumin seeds. Boil and cool completely before pouring over the olives and sealing.

Chillies in oil

This chilli-infused oil is useful to pour on top of pickles or chutneys before sealing them. It also makes a fiery oil for stir-frying or marinating.

Makes approximately 2 × 250 ml bottles

500 ml vegetable oil

6 bird's eye chillies

2 cinnamon sticks

Place the oil in a saucepan. Prick the chillies with a needle and place in the oil. Heat over a medium heat for 10 minutes, making sure the oil does not boil over. Remove from heat and pour into warm, sterilised jars. Add the cinnamon stick, and seal. Store for 1 month before opening.

Button mushrooms in oil

Makes approximately 2 × 750 g jars

1 kg button mushrooms,
  wiped clean

1 litre white wine vinegar

3 fresh bay leaves

3 cloves garlic, peeled
  and quartered

1 tablespoon sea salt

olive oil

Place the mushrooms, vinegar, bay leaves, garlic and sea salt in
a preserving pan and slowly bring to the boil. Cook for about 10
minutes. Remove from heat. Use a slotted spoon to take out the
mushrooms, then drain them in a sieve, reserving the garlic and bay
leaves. Pour a little oil in the bottom of a preserving jar and add the
mushrooms, garlic and bay leaves. Top up with extra oil to cover.

Seal and then refrigerate until ready to use. Alternatively
the filled jars can be sterilised in a water bath for 30 minutes
(see pages 9–10).

Chargrilled asparagus in oil

Serve this preserve on an antipasto platter scattered with a little fresh chopped parsley.

Makes approximately 1 × 850 g jar

2 cups white wine vinegar

2 cups water

2 bunches asparagus, trimmed

3 cloves garlic, peeled and sliced

300–500 ml olive oil

Bring the vinegar and water to the boil in a saucepan. Preheat a grill pan and cook the asparagus for a couple of minutes on each side to char it. Transfer immediately to the vinegar bath and leave for 3 minutes. Remove from heat and pack into sterilised jars with the garlic. Cover completely with olive oil and seal. Store in a cool dark place for 2 months before using.

Cherries in brandy

Great served with custard and a slice of sponge cake drizzled with a little of the cherry brandy liquid.

Makes approximately 2 × 500 g jars

1 kg cherries

1 litre brandy

150 g caster sugar

Trim half the stalk from each cherry and prick fruit all over with a needle (this will help the juices to flavour the brandy). Pack into sterilised preserving jars and cover with brandy. Add sugar, distributing it evenly among the jars. Seal and store in a cool dark cupboard for 6–8 weeks or longer. Shake the jars occasionally.

Peach and strawberry Melba

This delicious preserve is perfect with ice cream
or served with a cream-filled sponge.

Makes approximately 3 × 250 g jars

500 g strawberries, hulled

6 firm white peaches

1 cup water

¼ cup freshly squeezed
lemon juice

¼ cup light corn syrup

1¾ cups sugar

50 ml Grand Marnier or other
orange liqueur

Blend the strawberries in a food processor until smooth. Plunge
peaches in a bowl of very hot water, leave for 4 minutes and then
peel off the skins. Cut peaches in half, take out the stones and slice
flesh thinly.

Heat the water, lemon juice, corn syrup and sugar together in
a pan over a gentle heat, stirring until the sugar has dissolved. Stir in
the Grand Marnier and the strawberry puree. Cook for 2 minutes. Add
the peaches and simmer for about 20 minutes. Remove from heat and
pour into warm, sterilised jars leaving approximately 1 cm at the top.
Seal and place jars in a water bath for 30 minutes (see pages 9–10).
Remove and cool before labelling.

Preserved sticky toffee figs

This is one of the most special preserves you can make in fig season – a sweetmeat treat with coffee, or after dinner, or any time!

1 kg purple figs
2 cups water
4 cups sugar

3 tablespoons white wine vinegar
grated peel of 2 lemons

Gently prick the figs all over with a fine skewer. Place the water, sugar, vinegar and lemon peel in a preserving pan. Stir over a low heat until the sugar has dissolved. Bring to the boil and cook for 10 minutes. Add the figs and cook for 1 hour. Remove from heat and cool. Drain figs, reserving the liquid. Place figs on a wire rack on a baking tray and dry in a fan-forced oven (defrost mode, 85–90°C) for 4 hours. Remove.

Repeat the drying process for 3–4 hours the following day. (In summer the figs can be dried outside in the sun, but don't forget to protect them from birds and insects!)

Carefully place figs in single layers in airtight containers and store in a cool, dark place.

Candied oranges and lemons

These are lovely served on top of cakes or citrus tarts.

1 orange, washed
1 lemon, washed

2 cups white granulated sugar
1 cup water

With a very sharp knife, cut the orange and lemon into paper-thin slices. (A very sharp serrated edge knife works well.) The slices should be even in size and thickness. Carefully remove any pips and discard the end slices.

Place the sugar and water in a shallow, wide saucepan or deep frying pan and heat over a low heat to a rolling boil without stirring. Simmer for 5 minutes, then turn the heat right down and add a single layer of citrus slices, cooking for 35–45 minutes until softened. Carefully remove with a slotted spoon and cool on a sheet of nonstick baking paper. Repeat this process until all the slices have been cooked.

When the slices are dry and have hardened (2–3 hours), sprinkle a little caster sugar over. Store in an airtight container or freezer.

Candied citrus peel

Great for decorating cakes and desserts, or adding to meat
stuffing. For a delicious after-dinner treat, dip the ends in
melted dark chocolate and leave to set.

1 thick-skinned orange, 1 lemon
and 1 pink grapefruit

4 litres of water

2 cups white granulated sugar

1 cup water

Cut the fruit in half and squeeze out the juice. Scoop out all the flesh,
leaving just the peel and pith. Slice the halves into 8–10 strips. Place
in a preserving pan with 2 litres of the water and bring to the boil.
Cook for 10 minutes. Drain, return to the pan with the remaining
2 litres of water and cook for a further 20 minutes. Drain.

Place the sugar and 1 cup of water in a preserving pan and cook
over a low heat to a rolling boil without stirring. Simmer for 5 minutes.
Turn up the heat, add the boiled peel and simmer for 45–60 minutes
until translucent. Remove peel with a slotted spoon and place on
a cake rack on a sheet of nonstick baking paper. Allow to air dry.

When the peel has dried and hardened (2–3 hours), sprinkle
a little caster sugar over and store in airtight containers.

Moroccan preserved lemons

This classic preserve is used in tagines, couscous and salads. To use the lemons, first cut the flesh away from the skin and discard, then cut up the softened peel and add to the recipe as directed.

Makes approximately 1 × 1 litre jar

1 kg lemons

75 g sea salt

2 large bay leaves

1 cinnamon stick

2 small fresh chillies

juice of 8–10 lemons

olive oil

Wash the lemons in hot water, rinse well and dry. Cut each lemon in quarters, lengthways. Place about 1 tablespoon of salt in the bottom of a sterilised preserving jar. Dip the lemon quarters into the remaining salt and carefully pack them into the jar. Add the bay leaves, cinnamon stick and chillies. Pour in enough lemon juice to cover the lemons. Top with a little oil, then seal.

Leave in a warm, sunny spot for 4–8 weeks before opening.

Tangelo curd

A tangelo is a cross between a pomelo and mandarin and has a short season so take advantage of it by making this lovely curd. Use it to fill cakes or tarts.

Makes approximately 3 × 250 g jars

125 g unsalted butter

250 g caster sugar

2 tablespoons finely grated tangelo zest

125 ml freshly squeezed tangelo juice (2 tangelos approx)

4 egg yolks

1 whole egg

Place a stainless steel bowl over gently boiling water (or use a double boiler) and melt the butter and sugar together until dissolved. Add the zest and juice to the butter mixture and stir well. Beat the yolks and whole eggs together. Remove bowl from heat and strain eggs into the butter mixture. Return to heat and stir continuously until mixture will coat the back of a spoon (this may take about 15–20 minutes). The curd will thicken as it cools.

Remove from the heat, pour into warm sterilised jars and seal. Store in the refrigerator for up to 2 months.

Quince curd

This lovely, unusual curd is based on a quince cheese
made from slow-cooked quinces and sugar.

Makes 2 × 260 g jars

500 g quince cheese
(see page 135)

75 g unsalted butter

2 whole eggs, lightly whisked

Place the quince cheese in a small, heavy-based saucepan and
whisk in the butter over a low heat until combined. Over a very low
heat whisk the eggs into the quince mixture. Keep whisking for
5–8 minutes until combined. Remove from heat, pour into warm,
sterilised jars and seal. Store in the refrigerator for up to 4 months.

Passionfruit curd

Makes approximately 4 × 400 g jars

24 passionfruit, pulp scooped out
(300 g pulp approx)

2 cups caster sugar

250 g unsalted butter

8 eggs

Melt the butter and sugar together in a double boiler over gently boiling
water. When the sugar is dissolved, add the passionfruit pulp and stir
to heat through. Whisk the eggs together and strain into the mixture.
Cook for about 20 minutes, stirring constantly, until the mixture is thick
enough to coat the back of a wooden spoon. Cool a little then pour
into warm, sterilised jars and seal. Store in the refrigerator for up
to 2 months.

Lime curd

Makes approximately 3 × 250 g jars

125 g unsalted butter

1½ cups sugar

125 ml freshly squeezed lime juice

1 tablespoon finely grated lime zest

4 egg yolks

1 whole egg

In a double boiler over gently boiling water melt the butter and sugar together until dissolved. Stir in the lime juice and zest and heat through. Whisk the egg yolks and whole egg together in a bowl and strain into lime mixture. Cook for about 20 minutes, stirring constantly, until the mixture is thick enough to coat the back of a wooden spoon. Cool a little, then pour into warm, sterilised jars and seal.

Store in the refrigerator for up to 2 months.

Quince cheese

This is lovely served with a cheese platter
or with pears or apples.

Makes approximately 2.5 kg

1.5 kg quinces, washed
1 lemon

4 cups sugar

Preheat oven to 180°C.

Roast the quinces in an oven for 1–1½ hours until soft. Take out
of oven and remove the pips, core and skin. Blend the flesh in a food
processor and measure the puree (there should be about 4 cups).
Grate the rind of the lemon and squeeze out the juice. Add to the
quince puree with the sugar and leave overnight in a bowl.

Place in a preserving pan and cook over a low heat for
45–60 minutes until very thick. Spoon into a mould lined with lightly
oiled cling film. (A round cake tin or oblong bread tin can be used
to shape the cheese.) Cover and set aside to cool. Cut and pack
into airtight containers.

Store in a cool, dark cupboard for up to 12 months.

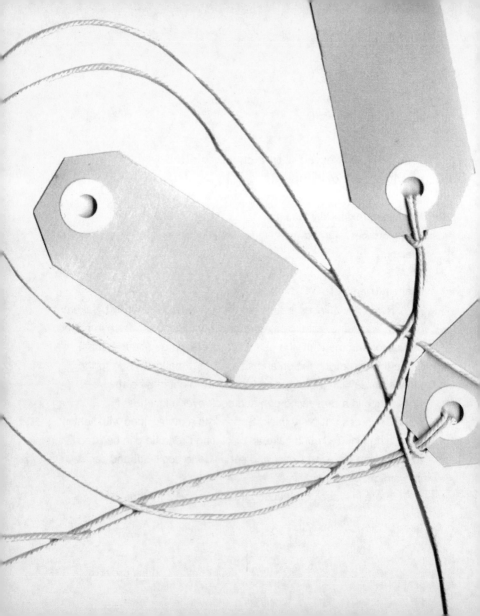

Index

Also available from Penguin Books

The Juice Book contains over 100 recipes for what has
to be the easiest and tastiest way to increase your vitamin
and mineral intake and boast your energy – juices!

Covering fruit juices, veggie juices, smoothies and special
energy and detox drinks, this book has a juice for every time
of day. Also included is information on equipment, sourcing the
best ingredients and nutrition – ensuring that you get the most
out of your juices. Make the recipes provided in the book,
then use them to create your own favourite juice.

www.penguin.com.au